The
Zebra Finch

An Owner's Guide To

A HAPPY HEALTHY PET

Howell Book House

Howell Book House
Hungry Minds, Inc.
909 Third Avenue
New York, NY 10022
www.hungryminds.com

For general information on Hungry Minds books in the U.S., please call our Consumer Customer Service department at 800-762-2974. In Canada, please call (800) 667-1115. For reseller information, including discounts and premium sales, please call our Reseller Customer Service department at 800-434-3422.

Library of Congress Cataloging-in-Publication Data

Vriends, Matthew M., 1937
The zebra finch: an owner's guide to a happy, healthy pet/ Matthew Vriends.
p. cm
Includes bibliographical references.

ISBN: 0-87605-525-0

1. Zebra Finch   I. Title.
SF473.Z42V75   1997-
636.6'862—dc21   97-22053
                CIP

Manufactured in the United States of America
10 9 8 7 6 5

Series Director: Ariel Cannon
Series Assistant Director: Jennifer Liberts
Book Design: Michele Laseau
Cover Design: Iris Jeromnimon
Illustration: Laura Robbins
Photography:
  Cover by B. Everett Webb
  Back cover and inset by Eric Hansenko
  Joan Balsarini: 82
  Michael DeFraitas: 5, 12, 16, 17, 27, 30, 37, 53, 66, 75
  Eric Hansenko: 2-3, 19, 24, 26, 39, 42, 46, 57, 58, 63, 78-79, 105, 107, 113
  Matthew Vriends: 6, 8, 14, 15, 25, 54, 61, 72, 80, 89, 92, 98, 100, 106, 113, 114, 116, 117, 119, 120
  B. Everett Webb: 7, 22-23, 40, 50, 65, 109, 112, 115, 116, 118, 122
Production Team: Robyn Burnett, Kathleen Caulfield, and David Faust

Contents

Welcome

to the

World

of the

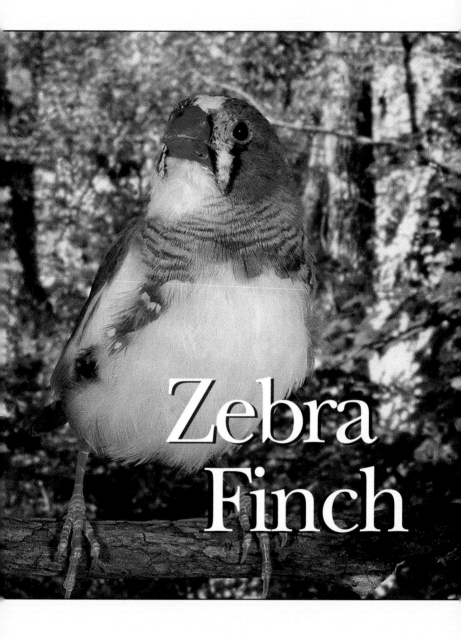

part one

Zebra Finch

External Features of the Zebra Finch

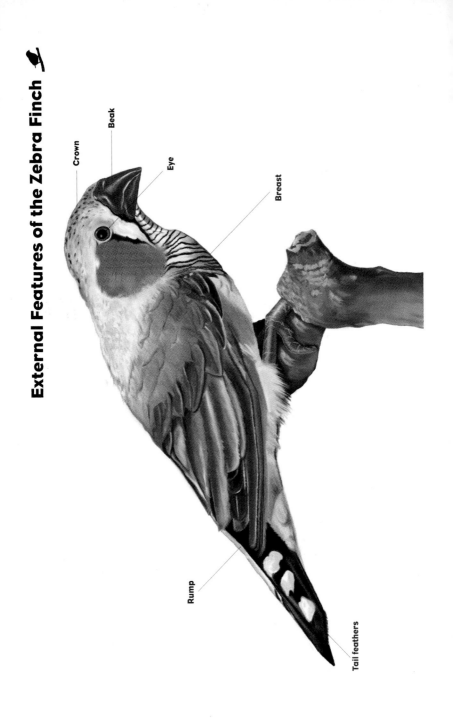

Crown

Beak

Eye

Breast

Rump

Tail feathers

What
Is a
Zebra Finch?

Zebra Finches belong to the subfamily *Estrildinae* of the family *Estrildidae*. Scientifically, the Zebra Finch is most widely recognized as *Poephila guttata castanotis* or *Poephila guttata*. *Poephila* is derived from the Greek poe = grass, and philos = to love, meaning "fond of grass" (which refers both to their method of nest construction and to grass seeds, which constitute a major part of their diet in the wild). The word *guttata* is derived from the Latin *gutta*, meaning spot or drop; *guttata* thus means: "spotted," referring to the drop-like markings on the flanks. *Castanotis* is derived from the Greek *castanon* = chestnut, and the Greek *otos*, genitive of ous = ear, and means (more or less) "with a chestnut colored ear."

Welcome to the
World of the
Zebra Finch

The subfamily *Estrildinae* is contained within the suborder of songbirds (*Oscines*), a branch of the extensive order of perching birds (*Passeriformes*). Australian Grass Finches, Waxbills, Mannikins, Munias and related species in the *Estrildinae* family were once all known as weaver finches, as they had many points in common with the true weavers (family *Ploceidae*). However, research into these matters has shown that the estrildid finches, including Zebra Finches, Gouldian Finches and similar species, possess several traits that are quite different to those of the weavers. These include such things as the anatomical structure of body organs (the syrinx, or voice box, for example) and behavior (particularly with regard to reproductive behavior). Reclassification has also been influenced by differences in general anatomy, feather structure and ecological considerations.

Zebra Finches use grass for nest contruction and eat the seeds.

Zebra Finches versus Weaver Finches

So why aren't Zebra Finches true weavers? In the true weavers (*Ploceidae*), the males begin nest construction by first weaving a few grass blades or stems around a twig before forming a ring-shaped construction which serves as the main framework of the nest. The roof is started next, followed by the rest of the outside. Lastly, attention is given to the lining of the nest. The males build several nests before they start courting the hens with song. The impressed hen will then choose what she thinks is the most appropriate nest in which to rear a family.

The estrildines, including Zebra Finches and other Australian, Asian and African finches, take a completely different approach to nest construction. They build the base first, usually a saucer- or bowl-shaped construction in the fork of a tree or among the dense foliage of a shrub. The side and the roof are added later, but there is never any true weaving as demonstrated by the weavers. It is thus better to include the estrildines among the grass and parrot finches (*Erythrurini*).

This Red Bishop is a true weaver; these finches are different anatomically, behaviorally and ecologically from estrildines, like the Zebra Finch family.

Zebra Finch Subspecies?

New species or subspecies are regularly being named, either as new species are discovered or as species are reclassified. Of course this causes continual changing of the scientific names which can be confusing if you do not keep up to date.

The Zebra Finch occurs throughout the continent of Australia and many ornithologists have recognized distinctive color variants from area to area. They designated these color variants subspecies within the

Welcome to the
World of the
Zebra Finch

species, and older literature may recognize up to seven of these false species. It is now generally recognized that all these varieties are in fact taxonomically identical though there are some obvious color differences. An Australian ornithologist, Dr. J.A. Keast, proved beyond doubt there are no subspecies of the Zebra Finch in Australia, however unlikely this may seem in such a large territory. One possible explanation for this unlikely act is that frequent droughts on the continent, especially in central Australia, force birds to migrate in search of water; causing a regular mixing of different bird populations, leading to a standardization of type.

Different markings do not necessarily mean different species. Here a male and female display different coloring.

Most modern bird books now list the classification of the Australian Zebra Finch as *Poephila guttata*. Within this single species there is a wide variety of markings, beak color and size.

There is an officially recognized subspecies that lives on some of the Indonesian Lesser Sunda Islands, including Timor and Flores, Letti, Sermatta, Luang and the Moa Islands. The color of this subspecies is brownish-yellow, and the top and sides of the head are darker than in the Australian race. The females of the Timor subspecies also have a darker breast and back.

It is interesting to note that the French ornithologist, Vieillot, who quite probably had Zebra Finches in his own aviaries, described the only recognized subspecies of Zebra Finch (the Indonesian race) rather than the Australian form; he made a mistake however, as he states that he was describing the Australian bird!

Description of the Zebra Finch

The male or cock is mainly softly grayish (gray-blue head and neck, gray-brown back), with a conspicuous orange or chestnut cheek patch, bordered below the eye with a narrow, black vertical line ("tear"). A further narrow black line edges the base of the beak, and the area between the two black lines is white. The wings are dark gray-brown. The throat and upper part of the breast are marked with horizontal dark gray, wavy lines that are bordered below with a wider breast band that runs across the width of the chest. The lower underside is beige-white, the flanks orange-red with round white spots. The tail is black with white diagonal bands. The rump and the under tail coverts are white. The beak is coral-red, the eyes red, the feet orange-brown.

> **WHAT'S IN A NAME?**
>
> **English name:** Zebra Finch
> **Scientific names:** *Poephila guttata castanotis, Poephila guttata, Taeniopygia guttata*
> **Other English names:** Chestnut Finch, Chestnut-eared Finch, and Spotted-sided Finch
> **French name:** Diamant Mandarin
> **German name:** Zebra Fink
> **Dutch name:** Zebravink

The signature chestnut cheek patch is evident on this pied male Zebra Finch.

The female, or hen, is gray above with a light gray (sometimes almost white) ear spot. The area between the black tear-line and the narrow black line round the

Welcome to the
World of the
Zebra Finch

base of the beak is white, as in the cock. The throat, neck, chest and sides are gray; the underside white-beige. The tail is similar to that of the cock, as are the white rump and under tail coverts. The beak is a much lighter red color than that of the cock; the eyes are red, the feet orange-yellow.

The attentive Zebra Finch observer will notice that there are some variations of the above descriptions among domestic stock. For example, domesticated birds have dark brown, rather than red eyes. The gray in the cock of domesticated gray Zebras (called "normals" by breeders) is more brownish. The underside of the wild hen is frequently much paler than that of the domesticated counterpart and the same can be said about the cheeks. Domesticated birds are also usually longer and more robust than wild specimens.

Notice the differences between the male and female Zebra Finch. (The female is on the right.)

The young or hatchlings already bear a resemblance to adult hens; only the black lines around the cheeks and beak are missing, and this area is colored gray rather than white. Hatchlings have pink (flesh-colored) skin, with or without sparse white down; the beak is horn-colored. In 3 weeks the skin gradually darkens, and a week later is almost black. In about 12 days the beak is quite black. The primaries appear after 7 days, the tail feathers on the tenth day and small contour feathers on the eleventh to twelfth days. The veins on the primaries can be seen at this time.

The size of the Zebra Finch's body is approximately 4–4.3 inches (10–11 centimeters); the tail 1.75 inches (3.5 centimeters), and the wings 2.125 inches (5.3 centimeters).

Zebra Finches forage mostly on the ground, less often in trees and shrubs. They do not walk like a starling, but hop like a sparrow with both feet together. Their flight is rapid, relatively direct and slightly undulating. They are capable of flying considerable distances without stopping to rest.

chapter 2

Zebra Finches
in the **Wild**

In the wild the Zebra Finch is common and widespread over most of the Australian continent. It is absent only from coastal northern Australia, Cape York peninsula, the extreme southeast (including Tasmania) and the rainforests of the extreme southwest.

Denser populations occur commonly in the more arid areas, but are also present in coastal areas, especially after long periods of inland drought. I have frequently seen flocks of one hundred or more birds in the regions of Brisbane and Townsville (Queensland), Campbelltown (New South Wales), Roebuck Bay and Carnarvon (Western Australia).

A subspecies of the Zebra Finch is, as I mentioned in chapter 1, also found on some of the Lesser Sunda Islands; the scientific name of this bird is *Poephila guttata guttata*.

Field Biology

As long as adequate supplies of water and food are available, the Zebra Finch is relatively sedentary in its habits. In other words, it stays put as long as conditions are good. However, the nature of the Australian climate is such that drought can occur in almost any region at almost any time. The climate is theoretically cyclic, but in reality, wildlife has to be able to adapt to any sudden emergency. Unseasonable droughts in one area mean that the normally sedentary Zebra Finches must move to more favorable areas. These local migrations mean that separate geographical flocks of birds meet up at regular intervals and are very likely to interbreed. This means that all populations eventually get together with all other populations over periods of years, resulting in a sort of natural standardization of type.

Because the continental race of Zebra Finches occurs over much of the Australian mainland (climate and topography can vary greatly over various parts of the continent), not all populations of Zebra Finches have the same lifestyle all the time. As an example, let us look at the life of Zebra Finches living in parts of central Australia. They may inhabit this area in favorable times but must nearly always head for more suitable areas during the summer drought. In such cases the birds may have to migrate almost to coastal areas in search of adequate water and food. Much of central Australia is rocky, but Zebra Finches may congregate in stands of scrub (known to Australians as mulga) or in the spinifex (a kind of grass with wiry stems), where they can take shelter from the hot sun, build their breeding nests or roost either among the foliage or in nests that are specially constructed for that purpose.

Welcome to the
World of the
Zebra Finch

During my visits to these habitats, I observed large numbers of Zebra Finches, although the conditions could not have been described as ideal (little water, inadequate nesting facilities, etc.). We must not forget, however, that Zebra Finches drink much in the manner of pigeons and doves, by sucking the water rather than scooping like most birds. This gives them the possibility of sucking up dew drops in the early mornings. Moreover, Zebra Finches have a lower metabolic rate than many other (non-Australian) birds and thus require less water. They also excrete less water in their droppings and are capable of consuming some brackish water without apparent ill effects.

This richly planted aviary is quite a departure from the sparsely vegetated savanna that is the Zebra Finch's home in the wild.

European settlement during the last 200 years has also had a beneficial effect on Zebra Finches, as well as many other forms of wildlife in the central areas of Australia. The installation of dams, bores, troughs and drains for irrigation and stock (cattle, sheep, horses) watering has allowed many species of birds to survive in large numbers in areas where this would previously not have been possible. Difficulties are experienced only by birds living in the real outback, or never-never (described by some Australians as the land that God forgot), which have to migrate to more favorable areas when times become desperate.

Large numbers of Zebra Finches may also be seen in the more inhabited areas of eastern, southeastern and southwestern Australia, where they occur in parks, gardens and plantations. Such birds have lost much of their natural fear and have become as cheeky as House Sparrows (Passer domesticus), which were introduced into Australia around 1850 and have spread throughout the continent.

FOOD FOR ZEBRA FINCHES IN THE WILD

Like the vast majority of Australian grass finches, Zebra Finches are basically, but not exclusively, seed eaters. In addition to half-ripe and ripe grass seeds (both wild and cultivated varieties) they will eat the seeds of many other plants as well as a variety of small insects. Several times I have observed Zebra Finches feeding on termites, small moths and flies (which they sometimes caught in flight); in addition to seeking insects on the ground, they also sought them among the foliage of trees and shrubs, where a quantity of larvae (caterpillars and grubs) are taken. Although they do not take so many insects outside the breeding season, hatchlings are fed almost exclusively on insects for the first few days of their lives.

In the wild, Zebra Finches prefer grass seeds, but will supplement their diets with insects and seeds of other plants.

Zebra Finch Calls

Zebra Finches are far from quiet, and although the characteristic, monotonous "tin-trumpet" call of this charming little bird can hardly be called a song, it isn't unattractive. The cock birds can sometimes be heard, especially in the evening, uttering a sort of short solo song.

The most important call, named the "identity call" by my friend, the late Dr. Karl Immelmann, is a nasal, trumpet-like "tiah." This is the species' most common

Welcome to the
World of the
Zebra Finch

vocalization both in the wild and in the cage and aviary. Individual birds use the call as well as large groups, usually in flight, and I have seen and heard groups of forty to one hundred birds using the call. Should one of the birds from the group lag behind, then the call becomes conspicuously more urgent in tone. During the breeding season this call can be continuously heard near the nesting sites as pairs keep contact with each other. In the case of approaching danger, the call becomes more penetrating and urgent.

Zebra Finches use a variety of calls to communicate with others in their group.

Dr. Immelmann also recognized a "communication call," similar to the "tiah" but softer and perhaps resembling a repetitive "tet, tet." In my opinion this call is not as urgent or alarming as the "tiah" and is used in smaller groups of, say, ten to twenty birds, and especially by pairs in flight. During mating, this call is also used but is even softer and occasionally sounds as if it is being uttered with difficulty. The call is often used by the cock as he spreads his tail to display the "zebra" markings of his rump and is thus designed to impress the female. Later this action may be used to reassure the hen during nest building or incubation.

Another call, a hissing "wssst" likened by Immelmann to the ripping of a piece of cotton cloth, is used by birds to warn off other birds, both of their own and other species, that come too close to their nesting sites.

Finally, there is the song, or what bird fanciers describe as the song. The song consists of series of harsh, low, nasal trills of up to 2 seconds in duration. Immelmann once compared these with "stomach talking," something that I find difficult to agree with. It must be noted here that this song, frequently heard in captive birds, is hardly ever heard in the wild except with males that do not have partners.

Courtship and Mating

Before actual copulation, the cock courts the hen with an attractive little dance. It is a rather simple dance when compared to that of other Australian grass finches and consists of the cock springing from twig to twig in the vicinity of the hen. At the same time, the cock points his beak in the direction of the hen, sometimes even rubbing his beak against hers. The cock's tail is also regularly bent in the direction of the hen, sometimes so it passes over her body. The hen usually perches quietly on a twig and allows the performance to proceed. (I rarely saw the hen playing a great part in the ceremony.)

Many scientists believe that Zebra Finches in the wild mate for life.

Sometimes the hen flits off to another perch and the cock continues the hopping performance as he follows her, his movements rapid and constant, so that a certain rhythm is followed. During the display, the feathers of the crown, the sides of the head, the cheeks and even the belly are regularly fluffed out. After some time the hen, if receptive, will respond by rapidly raising and lowering her tail; a sign that she is ready to mate.

Welcome to the
World of the
Zebra Finch

Pairing usually takes place on the ground, on a large stone, on rocks or in trees or shrubs with a large amount of dead wood so that the foliage does not get in the way. Copulation may occur several times during the mating period.

Whether Zebra Finches pair for life or regularly change partners is a point that is still not definitively determined by ornithologists, but most do believe that pairing is for life. In the cage or aviary this is of course not the case, especially with regard to the "forced" matings required for color breeding. It is generally accepted that pairs and groups of Zebra Finches stay together even outside the breeding season, sharing all of their daily activities, mutually preening and even sleeping in pairs in their special roosting nests. I have occasionally seen pairs outside the breeding season disappearing into their brooding nests in order to avoid the hot midday sun!

The Nest of the Zebra Finch

The building of their amazing nests is one of the most fascinating things about Zebra Finches.

Zebra Finches seem to have no special preference for nesting sites. I have seen nests in the most amazing places, but generally they build their nests in the thick foliage of small trees and shrubs. I often found nests in thorn scrub, and it is interesting to observe that in southwestern Australia, Zebra Finches almost exclusively use the thorny shrub *Hakea preissi* in which to build. Such a nesting site gives good protection against predatory birds and other animals. In the eastern areas, the birds often use introduced shrubs, including brambles, roses and citrus trees. Zebra Finches may also nest on the ground, among grass tussocks, in hollow limbs and in termite mounds. In Queensland and central Australia, I have even found nests in abandoned rabbit burrows!

Zebra Finches like to recycle nest material and will demolish one nest in order to construct another. In some cases they will use old nests again, and I have often found completely new pairs laying their eggs in long abandoned nests. Young pairs may even use the nests in which they were born when their parents "move out," and with marked (banded) birds this has been proven. Nests are occasionally found in the eaves of houses and other buildings, in abandoned vehicles, old tin cans, cooking vessels and so on! The height of the nest from the ground does not seem to be a major concern and may range from ground level to higher than 25 feet (approximately 8 meters).

Zebra Finches are able to use whatever material is at hand to build their nests.

The nest is a simple construction; nest material includes grass, moss and feathers. There are no hard and fast rules, and research has shown me that the main nest material used will depend on what is available in the habitat. Green grass may be used as well as dried grass, and in the absence of grass, small twigs may be taken. The nest is lined especially with small down feathers and I have often also found rabbit hairs, sheep wool, moss and small twigs.

Some birds, interestingly, hardly build a nest, using the old nests of Zebra Finches or other birds, including other grass finches and swallows, which they refurbish. Although both sexes will collect nesting materials, it is usually the cock that collects most of these, while the hen concerns herself mainly with the inner nest

Welcome to the
World of the
Zebra Finch

architecture. In the drier areas of central Australia I noted that both sexes were concerned with building the whole nest; perhaps a reflection on the urgency of completing a brood during the short wet season when adequate food and water is available.

In areas where plenty of water and food are available over longer periods, the nest takes 13 to 15 days to build, whereas when both birds build in a hurry it can take as little as 3 to 6 days.

Social Behavior of the Zebra Finch

Zebra Finches are extremely social birds. This is evident in their tendency to live in groups of forty to one hundred or more individuals. During the afternoon, the birds congregate together at a certain site in order to sing together and mutually preen. At dusk, the same birds huddle together to roost for the night at the roosting sites. In severe drought, groups can congregate together, forming flocks of one thousand or more individuals; these groups can, unfortunately, cause enormous damage if they should descend onto cultivated areas (especially seed crops).

During breeding times the large groups split up into smaller parties of five to twenty pairs, but they always remain in contact with the other groups. It is interesting to note that rarely is more than one nest (plus a roosting nest) to be found in the same tree or shrub; it can thus be surmised that each pair has its own mini-territory and therefore a certain amount of "privacy." In the more arid zones, however, where nesting sites may be scarce, a different situation arises, and sometimes ten to twenty nests may be found in the same tree or shrub.

Members of the group always keep in some form of contact with each other. Immelmann once told me that the birds certainly can recognize each other from their calls, and while neighbors may freely visit each other's nests, strangers are driven energetically away.

Most members of the colony congregate together at water sources several times a day in order to drink, bathe and mutually preen. Similarly they fly in groups to the feeding grounds, which may be up to 100 meters away from the nesting sites.

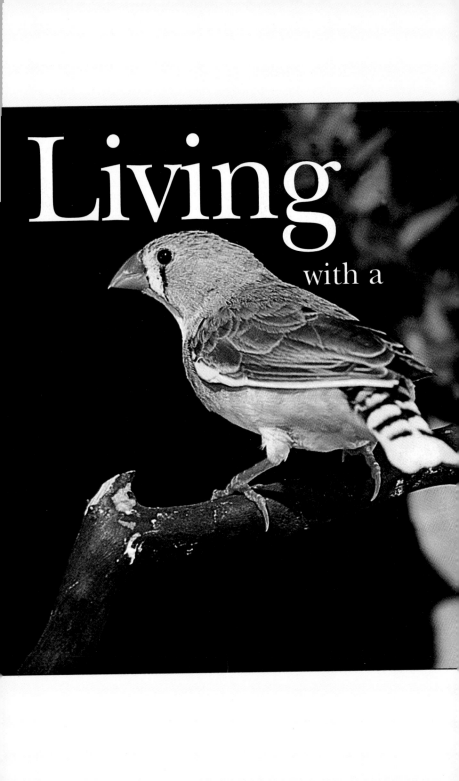

Living

with a

part two

Zebra
Finch

chapter 3

The **Zebra Finch** in **Captivity**

We can assume that Zebra Finches have been known in Europe for about 200 years and were probably imported even earlier than Budgerigars (parakeets). Vieillot, a French ornithologist, was perhaps the first person to keep and breed Zebra Finches in captivity.

Whatever the case, in 1872 the German magazine *Die Gefiederte Welt* reported about Zebra Finch breeding as though it was the most usual thing in the world. In his 1879 book "Prachtfinken" (Estrildid Finches), the well-known German ornithologist and aviculturist, Dr. Karl Russ, stated that "the experience derived from breeding Zebra Finches is fundamental to the breeding of all other cage birds." The English aviculturist C.W. Gedney gave a comprehensive description of the care and breeding of Zebra

Finches in his book "Foreign Cage Birds," also published in 1879.

The late Mr. H. Rensenbrink of the famous Artis Zoo in Amsterdam told me that the first Zebra Finches (still known then under the scientific name of *Taeniopygia castanotis*) arrived there in 1859. They were given the name "Mandarin Amadina," which was probably derived from the French "Diamant Mandarin." Mr. Rensenbrink was unable to tell me the exact date of the first specimens arriving in Europe but did find a report that Vieillot had bred them in Paris.

Today, breeding Zebra Finches is common and relatively easy. This was not the case when this bird was first introduced to Europe.

The former director of the Burger's Zoo (Arnhem, The Netherlands), Dr. R.A. Th. van Hooff, told me that the first Zebra Finches in the west were brought to London. "But when this occurred cannot be determined, since it concerned just a little insignificant bird. The zoo in Antwerp (Belgium) probably got one soon after London, as did Artis, while it is probable that Berlin (Germany) had one of the first. As far as I can trace back, our park received its first Zebra Finches in 1928; in 1929 and 1930 we bred them. Where and when the first was bred is extremely difficult to say."

The Origins of Mutations
Zebra Finches became popular and desirable as breeding birds all over western Europe during the latter half

of the nineteenth century. Though it is still not known where and when the first Zebra Finch was bred in captivity, we do know that the first mutation, the white Zebra Finch, was bred in Australia. As reported by C. af Enehjelm of Helsinki in his article in *Foreign Birds* (September, 1956), the white color first appeared during 1921 in a community aviary owned by A.J. Woods of Sydney. The three white birds were sold by Woods to a fellow citizen named H. Lyons who standardized the mutation and bred several hundred birds. The first white Zebra Finches arrived in Europe in the mid 1930s. The silver (or dilute normal) mutation also originated in Australia, and the first examples reached the western world before the second World War.

The white color was the first mutation to be bred in captivity.

Enehjelm thought it possible that the first fawn or normal brown mutation was bred in Australia, but C. Stork puts this down to F. Mills of Johannesburg, South Africa (1942). Enehjelm also stated that the first pied or variegated Zebra Finch was hatched in the aviaries of U. Nilsson (Copenhagen, Denmark) in the early 1930s. Whitehouse, of Brisbane, Australia, first saw the chestnut-flanked white Zebra Finch in the wild and in 1937 was fortunate in producing the mutation in his captive breeding stock. However, only females were produced at first and it was several more years before he succeeded in producing a male. This was one of the last important mutations to become known in Europe.

Common Color Mutations

Presently, there are forty or more recognized color mutations, and at least ten more are theoretically possible. To date, more color mutations have arisen in Zebra Finches that in any other finches. This is probably because these birds have been kept in captivity longer and these captive populations have become fairly inbred, allowing for the expression of more unusual traits. In a wild population, unusual traits would be carried by individuals, but the genes for these traits would most likely be recessive and would be overwhelmed by the dominant genes. It is only in captivity and with careful breeding that such mutations can be reproduced with regularity and predictability. The most important color mutations are the following:

Today there are several different common color mutations.

White Zebra Finch   This mutation first arose in Australia in 1921. The white Zebra Finch is pure white, with no markings. Beak color can be used to distinguish the sexes (the male's beak is darker red than the female's). There is also an Albino mutation, though it remains very rare. In this mutation, the finch is pure white, but its eyes are red rather than dark brown.

Pied Zebra Finch   This variety was first bred in Denmark. Pied is recessive to gray. In the pied mutation, the pattern of the bird's feathers is irregular, with white and dark areas both present to more or less of a degree.

Fawn Zebra Finch   This is a warm brown shade, rather that the normal gray shade of the Zebra Finch's feathers. There is also a fawn pied, in which the bird's feathers are mixed fawn and white. This color was first discovered in Australia in 1927. The mutation is what is known as sex-linked; hens can inherit the mutation from a fawn cock, but fawn hens can only produce fawn sons. Hens cannot have the color hidden (split) but cocks can.

Silver Zebra Finch   In this mutation, the finch's feathers are a light shade of gray rather than the dark, camouflaging tone which is normal. This non–sex-linked mutation first turned up in Australia but was already known in the United States by 1938. The silver factor is dominant and can therefore not occur as split. However, the silver factor can occur as single factor (s.f.) and double factor (d.f.), although they show outwardly no major differences. The single factor is the most common.

Cream Zebra Finch   This arises from a combination of silver factor and fawn. It is thus both dominant and sex-linked.

Penguin Zebra Finch   Developed by the well-known English breeder J. Pope, this variety lacks the barring on the throat and breast, and is pure white from neck to vent. The lower belly and tail, however, are often difficult to get pure white. The gray color of the normal is replaced by silver-gray, and the hen has white cheeks.

Marked Zebra Finch   This beautiful sex-linked variety is creamy white in color (both cocks and hens). The black markings are retained and the cocks retain the orange flank marking.

OTHER MUTATIONS

In Europe, today, several attractive new color mutations are being bred. Among these are the orange-
breasted, which has a bright orange head and breast,
and the black-breasted, which has an orange head and
very dark brown breast.

The Zebra Finch as a Pet

The Zebra Finch has been a welcome addition to
aviaries for centuries, but today more and more people
are keeping Zebra Finches as pets. This charming little
bird is the most popular pet bird behind the budgie
and canary and are found in homes of people from
every walk of life. Why are birds in general, and Zebra
Finches in particular, becoming so popular? Could it
have something to do with their easy care, affectionate
natures and soothing calls? Or is it because people are
fascinated by animals, especially one like the Zebra
Finch, that has retained its natural behavior and
instincts during its coexistence with humans? For many
people, keeping birds allows them insight into the
wonderful, mysterious world of nature. In fact, these
are just some of the reasons people are keeping more
and more birds, and more and more Zebra Finches in
their homes.

WHY A PET BIRD?

Birds can live anywhere.   Although a full-grown
Scarlet Macaw will make noise, other birds, including
Zebra Finches, are quiet companions. Properly kept,
birds are a landlord's friend. They don't require a lot
of space, they don't make disruptive noises and they
don't "mark" the new carpet.

**Birds require consistent, but not constant, atten-
tion.**   A bird doesn't need to be walked three times a
day or get expensive professional training. A bird who
is well fed, kept in a large cage and properly cared for
will be happy with some quality attention every day.
Larger parrots will need more interaction, but finches
will be happiest when bonded with their mates rather

than their owners. This doesn't mean that they can be neglected! The more you put into your relationship with your finch the more you will get out of it.

Birds are great companions! People love the happy, chirpy personalities of their feathered friends. A pet bird can give your life extra meaning, as you care for and have a close connection with this wild creature that chooses to trust you. Many owners bond deeply with their birds. Sharing our lives with these pretty, cheerful animals is a reward to be savored. They are active and charming; their songs are fascinating and beautiful and their colors varied and enchanting.

Zebra Finches are friendly, attractive and easy to care for—perfect for the beginner.

So Why a Zebra Finch?

As I write these words, I am able to glance across the room to a cage standing on a small table. In the cage are two fluffy little gray balls of feathers squeezed tightly together on a perch—my two gray Zebra Finches fast asleep.

"What is it," I ask myself, "that attracts me and so many other bird lovers to Zebra Finches?" In response, one can summarize all of the marvelous qualities of these interesting birds: their attractive colors and patterns; their cheerful and friendly attitude; their readiness to breed (if properly managed, of course); their talent in nest building; their vivacity and their adaptiveness.

The size of a bird may also have something to do with it, and I can indeed understand that little mites like Zebra Finches are more attractive to many than an "overgrown" canary or budgie. The shape of a bird may also play a part. The round, chubby shape of the Zebra Finch has a cuteness that the slender form of other birds cannot rival. The quaint calls of excited male Zebras are another aspect of the birds that many owners find quite irresistible.

Yes, the Zebra Finch certainly has plenty of good qualities!

FINCHES AND CHILDREN

A mature youngster can learn to care for the bird, how to handle it properly and what it means to be responsible for the life of another being. A younger child can participate in caring for the bird by offering treats and helping parents feed the birds. Of course, a parent must always supervise the children in these activities. And, remember, parents are ultimately responsible for the birds' welfare. If your child forgets to feed the bird, you must do so. Children cannot be expected to take on adult responsibilities, and when they are, it is usually the bird who suffers. Find another way to take a stand on responsibility issues.

Have your children spend time each day talking quietly to the birds and observing them. If you are interested in breeding your birds, this can be a wonderful opportunity for a child to learn about avian reproduction and the miracle of life. Have your child keep a journal of the developing baby birds. Make this an opportunity for both you and your child to focus on the parental behavior and the growth and development of the offspring. Older children can even learn about the genetics behind breeding.

AN EDUCATIONAL HOBBY

Although Zebra Finches do not bond intensely with their human caretakers, the rewards of keeping Zebra Finches are many. Aviculture is a greatly rewarding hobby. You will be among friends: There are other eager and willing bird people around to swap secrets and trade stories. Aviculture is also a very educational pastime. There is always new material being written on all aspects of living with birds, and a multitude of magazines are dedicated to new developments in the field. Use your knowledge to bring other people into the fancy. Consider speaking to school or church groups, join a bird club and spread your knowledge and enthusiasm for the Zebra Finch far and wide!

Bringing Your
Zebra Finch
Home

Before you buy a Zebra Finch you should carefully consider your resources, living situation and commitment to caring for this little bird. Many beginners make the mistake of buying birds on impulse and then have difficulty accommodating them. Remember that any captive creature is totally at the mercy of  its owner. You must therefore be absolutely sure that you have the dedication and ongoing enthusiasm to assure the welfare of your birds. Do you have time each day to offer new food and water? Can you be sure to clean the cage thoroughly at least once a week? Do you have a chance to spend a little time with your birds each day, perhaps as you offer a piece of fruit or green leafy vegetable? If you can't be sure you'll have this time, perhaps you should wait to bring Zebra Finches into your life until you have time to enjoy them.

Grass finches, like Zebra Finches, Gouldian Finches and Diamond Finches, are the most popular finches today. Such birds are well suited for beginners as they have no great care demands and are cheerful, amiable companions. They are equally popular with more experienced aviculturists as they offer great opportunities for achieving interesting breeding results. In fact, most of the Australian grass finches are easy to care for and will be great pets for those who commit to caring for them.

Choosing Your Zebra Finch

When you buy your first Zebra Finch it's a good idea to take a more experienced bird owner with you to give you some tips in choosing your bird or birds. The practiced eye will more readily identify potential problems. Look at the feathers first: A sick bird will have feathers that are dull and parted. A good feather covering is important, but do not be too worried about damaged feathers that have resulted from overcrowding in stock cages or aviaries; the bird's plumage will vastly improve after the next molt as long as it has optimum housing and feeding conditions.

SIGNS OF HEALTH

When you set out to purchase your first Zebra Finch, make sure you know what to look for. Avoid birds that display any of the following symptoms:

listless demeanor
discharge from the eyes
dull feathers
continual sleeping
wet and dirty vent

Instead, seek a bird that is alert and interested in its surroundings. The feathers of a healthy bird should be full and shiny and the eyes should be clear and bright.

Do not choose any that peck excessively at their own plumage, or are continually scratching with the toes; these actions could indicate skin problems, among other things. Do not buy birds that are wet and dirty around the vent as this could indicate an intestinal infection. If at all possible, watch how the birds sleep. Healthy adult finches sleep with one leg pulled up and the beak tucked among the feathers. A very young finch will sleep with both feet on the perch, its head tucked under a wing. All Zebra Finches hunch down to help keep their feet warm and conserve energy (even in Australia the temperature can differ markedly between day and night), but do not buy birds that sit hunched up in a corner continually sleeping. Other signs of ill health include rapid breathing, puffed-out feathers and lack of interest in the surroundings.

The birds should be normally shaped with no evidence of deformities, especially of the beak and feet. The breast should be plump and full with no sign of a protruding breastbone. The eyes must be clear and bright, not watery; a bird with an eye infection will rub the eyes continually against perches and other surfaces. Beware of chills; non-acclimatized birds are especially susceptible.

A healthy Zebra Finch should be plump, active and alert.

Try to get the dealer (or local breeder or pet shop manager) to agree to exchange any bird that does not turn out to be the sex or quality you require.

How Many?

Zebra Finches are extremely social birds. In the wild they live in large groups and also have the companionship of a mate. Many scientists believe these little birds mate for life, and pairs are seen together even outside of the breeding season. Therefore, it is definitely better for your finch's comfort and happiness if your purchase a companion to keep your bird company. Although larger psittacine birds adapt quite well to living alone provided they are given enough attention by their owners, a life alone in a cage is not a good one for a finch. Besides, if one Zebra Finch is good, an active pair of these charming birds is certainly better!

What Does the Band Mean?

When you are looking at Zebra Finches, you will notice many are banded around one leg. The bands identify a certain breeder's stock, and because the numbers on the bands usually include the year of hatching, the band can help you determine your finch's age.

If you plan to start a breeding program with your Zebra Finches, the bands can help you tell the birds apart and select specific pairs for breeding. You will also need to learn how to do the banding yourself, as you will need to identify offspring. Ask for advice from breeders and members of your bird club about this and all breeding-related topics.

Transporting Your Zebra Finches

After choosing your birds, you will need to get them home safely. You may transport your finches in specially designed cardboard boxes (one bird in each box) if you are going only a short distance. If you are going a long way, a small transport cage made out of wood is ideal.

It is best to acquire your finches in the morning so that they will have as much of the day left as possible to eat, drink and get accustomed to their new home.

Birds in transport boxes will be in semi-darkness for a short time and will thus be quiet. It is not necessary to give water or food for journeys of half an hour or less. For longer journeys in a transport cage you can give the birds some seed or pellets and some soaked bread (instead of water that would only get spilled) on the floor so they can easily find it. To keep the birds quiet, you can cover most of the cage with a cloth or some thick wrapping paper. Make sure the birds are not subjected to strong drafts. Also, for obvious reasons, never leave birds (or any other animal, for that matter) inside a locked car on a hot day.

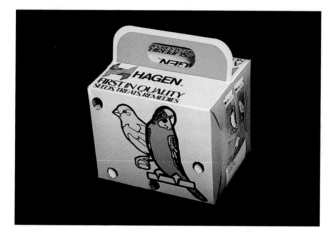

Bring your bird home from the pet store in a transport box like this one.

Get your birds to their destination as quickly as you can. Finches cannot go for very long without food and water (never more than 1 hour!). Remember that you can keep them happy with a spray of millet if necessary.

SHIPPING ARRANGEMENTS

If someone ships birds to you, be especially cautious if this is done in winter. Cold temperatures cause the temperature to drop inside the hollow bone structure of the birds. You have the natural tendency to put a cold bird up close to a toasty heater, but actually that is the most dangerous thing you could do. The air in the bones expands in response to the sudden increase in temperature, which causes the birds a lot of pain. It could even kill them! Instead, warm them up gradually. Better yet, wait until the weather is warmer to receive your bird.

When making shipping arrangements, remember that Zebra Finches need to eat every single day and they should always have access to seed, pellets and water.

Arriving Home

Your new birds will be understandably shy and nervous from the stress of being caught up and transported, so give them absolute peace and quiet in their quarantine cage or leave them alone in their transport cages for a few hours until they get a chance to recover.

Give them food that is familiar to them and room-temperature water. Cold water could bring about intestinal problems.

QUARANTINE CAGE

All new birds should spend a period of a least 3 weeks in a quarantine cage before being introduced to any existing stock you may have. You will thus help to prevent the spread of any diseases that may be incubating in the new birds. Birds that are still fit and well after the quarantine period are usually safe to introduce.

INTRODUCING YOUR NEW ZEBRA FINCH TO OTHER BIRDS

If your Zebra Finch will be living with other birds in a community aviary or large flight, take the time to make introductions thoughtfully. After your new Zebra Finch has had a chance to recuperate from the journey in private, you will need to introduce it to the other birds in your collection. Because Zebra Finches are social birds, the introduction of a new member of your community should rarely cause a problem.

Make sure your Zebra Finch has a mate before you include him in a community aviary. An extra male Zebra Finch, for example, could upset the whole population of a cage or aviary if he was no longer required for brooding.

Unfortunately, not all finch species get along with each other. (See chapter 9 for a list of compatible finches.) Not every finch species is suited to a communal aviary or large cage—especially if it includes only two breeding pairs. Zebra Finches, various Lonchura species and Diamond Firetail Finches, for example, will be forever battling if two couples are housed together. It is different if there are three or more pairs.

When the time comes to integrate new birds into the rest of your collection, place the newcomers, cage and all, into the aviary. Keep them inside the cage half a day, from 7 a.m. to 1 p.m. This way the birds can get used to one another before you release the newcomers. Then watch the situation closely. It can happen that the established group will not accept the newcomers, seeing them as a challenge to their territory.

It's best to have a companion for your Zebra Finch, even if you plan to keep it with other birds.

Watch what happens for a few days; if the rejection continues, remove the new birds and then reintroduce them gradually after another few days have passed. Generally, new birds won't cause problems in the aviary, provided it isn't overcrowded. Be aware, of course, that you shouldn't introduce new birds during the breeding season. You are really asking for trouble if you do that!

Above all, be aware of what's going on. Who are the bullies? Who gets it in the neck? Who needs extra food, more nesting material or a different partner? Don't leave anything to chance; act immediately if you think all is not well.

Zebra Finch Housing

Location of the cage is quite important. Be sure there is enough light and fresh air—but definitely no drafts! Avoid places that get direct sunlight; this can rapidly raise the temperature in the cage to dangerous levels.

CAGE SIZE

Zebra Finches and other finches are rather small, and people are tempted to think that they can be kept in small quarters. Not so. There should always be enough room for them to exercise adequately. Small quarters lead to fat and listless birds. Even the smallest finches should be given a cage of at least 30 inches long × 18 inches wide × 20 inches high (75 × 45 × 50 centimeters), and always housed in pairs if possible.

I prefer cages that are as long as they are wide, which would change the dimensions I just mentioned to 30 inches × 30 inches. Cages measuring 30 inches × 30 inches × 20 inches are appropriate for two pairs of different species. At that level of crowding, however, don't set your sights too high for breeding results.

TYPES OF CAGES

The best cage is the so-called box cage, which allows birds to feel the most protected and safe. A box cage has wire mesh only on the front. The sides, roof, floor and rear wall can be made of wood or other material. Paint the inside of the cage with a safe, lead-free, light-colored paint, that is easy to wash. For the outside, use any type of paint you wish. Over the floor, build a second floor of metal (zinc), hard-board, or the like, that can slide in and out. Then take a sheet of glass about 4 inches (10 centimeters) high and put it along the entire length of the cage at the bottom to prevent spills of seed hulls, sand and feathers. Make sure this sheet of glass is easy to remove. In the sidewall (and the rear wall too, if you like), install some doors so you can reach all areas of the cage. Ideally, the front of the cage also should be constructed so it can slide open; this helps simplify feeding and watering. There are ready-to-use mesh fronts in various sizes available in the better pet shops. You can hang a waterbottle or even the well-known plastic bath in one of the doors, although, regarding the latter, a flat earthenware dish set on the floor will also be appreciated.

> ## HOUSING OPTIONS
>
> A pair of finches will be happy in a roomy cage, provided there is enough room to exercise. If you are willing to go the extra mile, however, a bird room or aviary would offer ideal accommodations for your finches. Consider turning an existing room in your house into a bird room and building an attached aviary where the birds can venture when the weather is warm. Providing your birds with as natural an environment as possible will stimulate a variety of fascinating natural behaviors.

Another type of cage is the vitrine, which at this moment is very popular and often advertised in various bird magazines. Vitrines make excellent quarters, provided they are constructed correctly and are large enough. Zebra Finches are ideal birds for this type of housing.

The front of a vitrine is made of glass or Plexiglas. The sides and roof are made partially of wire mesh; these parts should be equipped with shutters to regulate fresh air and ventilation. There should be several doors in the sides to permit all necessary tasks. A vitrine is ideal for a living room, den or study. Add some suitable live plants and you will have a really attractive exhibit.

41

I recommend that the glass front slope, so the vitrine is wider at the bottom than at the top. This way, droppings and dirt are less likely to spoil the view. The glass front really should be removable, so it will slide out easily for cleaning. Make two parallel grooves on each side, so, before removing the glass plate, you can install a solid piece of cardboard or a similarly sized piece of glass to contain the birds. The bottom also should have a floor that can slide out as with a box cage.

Equip your Zebra Finches' cage with perches of various sizes and textures.

You can back-light the vitrine if you like. Some people decorate the walls with nature scenes, but I don't recommend this. You can become bored looking at these after awhile. The glass front, of course, gets dirty, and you need to wash it at least twice a week.

Equipping Your Facilities

Equip your cage properly. Furnish some live branches, placed in jelly jars filled with wet sand to keep them fresh. Have some containers solely for green food, and supply separate dishes for food, water and bathing. Also install several perches separated by appropriate distance.

PERCHES

You should get two different types of perches: anchored ones and swinging ones. The swinging perches are for play, the anchored ones are for resting and for mating during the breeding season.

Perches should be made of hardwood dowels that one slightly flattened on top. Hardwood is recommended because it is less likely to harbor lice and mites. The perches should not be too thin. They must be thick enough to keep the toes of resting birds from closing around them completely. Otherwise, the birds can't relax well. I suggest you get perches of different diameters. These help keep toenails trim and leg muscles limber. Don't use perch covers made from sandpaper; these cause little wounds on the foot and toes that often lead to infections.

Don't skimp on places to perch and sleep. You don't want your birds to get into fights over them. Don't install one perch on top of another. You don't want birds perching above to foul the ones below. For the same reason, don't install perches over food and water bowls or baths.

For natural perches, I recommend branches from fruit, willow, elderberry and sycamore trees. Remember to replace them regularly, because after awhile, cut branches lose their elasticity. If you have birds with quickly growing nails (Munia-species, for example), I recommend reeds and similar plants that help keep their nails trim. Rough stones (flagstones) serve the same purpose.

BIRD GRAVEL

Cover the floor with so-called "bird gravel" (sharp sand, often with charcoal, which somewhat combats hyperacidity and sweetens the stomach, and oyster shell, which supplies calcium) about 1 inch ($2\frac{1}{2}$ centimeters) deep and put some small stones (flagstones and such) on top.

FOOD AND WATER DISHES

Utensils come in many shapes, sizes and colors. The best ones are made of white porcelain or hard plastic, are oval, and measure about 4 inches (10 centimeters) in diameter. You can consider automatic feeders, provided they really work well. Automatic waterers or drinking vessels are good, too, and are really better than bowls because birds can't foul them. Large, glazed bowls or plastic containers are useful for sprouted seeds, universal or egg feed, and other supplements that are provided in small quantities to prevent spoilage. Separate vessels for grit and oyster shell must also be provided.

Place grit, egg and/or rearing food and other supplements in separate vessels. Cuttle bone should be hung against the outside wall of the cage. During the breeding season hang small baskets with nest-building material in the same place. You can also buy special racks for providing green food. Branches (with aphids—on roses!) and bunches of weeds (for seeds) can be put in flower pots filled with wet sand.

Check on the utensils daily. Fill food bowls daily and put fresh, clean water in dishes several times daily.

Bird Bath

Use flat bowls for bird baths. If you don't have them, you can adapt deeper bowls by putting flat stones or gravel in them. You want to prevent drowning, particularly of young birds.

Check the water in the bird bath several times daily and refill as necessary. Thoroughly rinse the bird bath every few days.

Lighting

Provide good lighting. Finches are just plain lovers of light. In fall and winter, when it gets dark early, provide extra light so birds can continue to eat and drink. Exotic finches should have at least 10 to 13 hours of light each day. Also, install a small night light (4 to 7 watts), so birds that fly up when they are startled can find their sleeping spots again. When you turn off the lights, dim them gradually.

HEATER

A heater that can provide the required temperature safely is very important! Most species, including Zebra Finches, cannot tolerate temperatures below 50 degrees F (10 degrees C). Keep alert to the weather forecast. You will need a thermometer to check the temperature and maintain it properly.

SHELTER

If you don't have the facilities to provide your birds with an opportunity for nesting in captivity, be sure to provide them shelter within their cages. Offer a small nesting box or enclosure that they can go into. This will make them feel much more secure and comfortable.

Maintenance

The importance of daily maintenance is twofold: Good hygiene will help keep your bird healthy, and daily contact with your bird will help it become more familiar with you. Food stuck on cage bars and on cage floors can attract all kinds of pests, water bowls contaminated with food and droppings can spread disease, and food that is unclean or less than fresh can make your bird ill. A daily maintenance routine will also help you make friends with your finch. Finches feel secure when they know what and who to expect. Establishing a daily routine and sticking to it will help your birds to become familiar with you and comfortable with your presence. Establishing a daily routine will prove to be helpful to you as you observe your birds for behaviors that could indicate health or other problems, monitor their activities and nests during breeding season and watch to make sure the young are developing healthily. Besides, isn't being around your birds what you got them for in the first place?

The following are chores that should be performed each day, at the same time, to keep your finches clean and healthy:

- Remove food dish and wash thoroughly. Offer fresh food, especially perishable food that has a limited life span outside of the refrigerator.

- Remove water dish; rinse thoroughly and refill with fresh water.

- Change paper in cage tray.

- In the evening, remove any uneaten perishable food. Check to make sure there is plenty of clean water. If not, rinse and refill the water bowl again.

- Observe your birds. Keep and eye out for any strange behavior, and report it to your veterinarian.

Spend quality time with your Zebra finch. This one is enjoying relaxing in his owner's hand.

Once a week, your finch's cage should be cleaned and scrubbed thoroughly. You will need a another (very simple) cage to keep the birds in while you perform this chore. As you are cleaning the cage, make sure that any food or debris that has fallen in the corners of the cage is removed. Scrub away any stuck-on food with an old toothbrush or steel wool. Clean the perches and any other cage equipment. Consider having at least two sets of food and water dishes and nest boxes so you can thoroughly clean one set while the other is being used. If you choose not to do this, make sure all cage accessories are thoroughly dry before being returned to the cage. Make sure the cage is dry before replacing your finches inside.

Catching and Handling Your Finch

You will need to catch and hold your finch when you move it from cage to cage, when you administer medication or perform any number of other day-to-day activities. Zebra Finch's beaks are not strong enough to inflict a serious bite wound, so it's not necessary to wear gloves when handling your birds. It's much easier to trap and catch your bird in a cage than in an aviary, especially after all the cage accessories have been removed. Once this has been done, you can corner and catch your bird with one hand, while keeping the other hand at the door to make sure the bird does not escape. Hold the bird gently in your hand with its wings folded. Your fingers will encircle its neck, but make sure you do not squeeze tightly. Use common sense and be gentle. Remember that your Zebra Finch is indeed a fragile creature!

If your Zebra Finch escapes, use its mate to bring it back to the cage.

If Your Finch Escapes

It can happen that a bird escapes. If it is one of a pair, then it shouldn't ordinarily be difficult to catch the escapee. Use a cage with a trap door and put the remaining partner of the pair in the closed part of the cage. Then put some seeds or pellets in the part with the trap door. The bird in the cage will send out contact calls and it won't be long before the escaped bird is attracted to the cage. When it observes its partner in the cage and discovers familiar food in the cage as well, it will return to captivity quickly. Even if the escapee isn't paired, another bird of the same species can still serve as bait. If two paired birds both escape, the situation is a bit more difficult. Still, the process is the same. You put another bird of the same species in the trap cage to attract one of the escaped birds, which then in turn serves as bait for the other.

If you don't have any success with the trap cage you have to wait until evening. Note precisely where the escaped Zebra Finch goes to sleep. Then shine a flashlight directly at the escaped bird. The sharp light seems to freeze the roosting bird in its resting place, and you can lift it off the branch by hand.

If a finch escapes from a cage, it is often enough to remove all other inhabitants temporarily from that cage and set it outside, with the door(s) open. Hunger and thirst will tend to drive the escapee back to the trusted cage after a few hours to take advantage of the food and water it finds there.

Quality Time

Put aside some time each day to spend with your Zebra Finch. The more time you spend with your birds, the more familiar with you they'll become and the more peacefully they'll let you observe and interact with them. The more familiar you are with your finch's routine, the more quickly you'll be able to recognize if something's wrong. Make it a point to know your bird's normal behavior and don't hesitate to call your avian veterinarian if you notice something amiss.

Finches are birds of routine. They feel most comfortable when surrounded by familiar sights and sounds. For this reason, always maintain the same appearance when working around finches. If you wear glasses, always wear them. If you wear a hat in winter, wear it in summer too. Wear a dust coat to protect your clothes and standardize your appearance. When it wears out, try to buy a replacement of the same color. Keep up this appearance whenever you do any work near the birds.

chapter 5

Feeding
Your
Zebra Finch

Food is a combination of materials that every organism requires for normal growth, reproduction, development and protection against diseases. It consists of a number of chemical components: proteins, carbohydrates, fats, vitamins, minerals and water.

Energy is derived from these sources. A deficiency of one or more of these constituents will result in bodily malfunctions. These malfunctions, or illnesses, can occur in a period as short as one week, or they may develop over a longer period of time. These malfunctions usually manifest themselves much faster in growing birds than in adults. A nutritional deficiency may be caused by a shortage of a particular element or a combination of different food items. Furthermore, it may be difficult to ascertain exactly which items these are.

A good diet is one that keeps a bird at an optimal standard of health, full of energy and "joie de vivre." A good diet also ensures a long, trouble-free life. We who keep birds must take full responsibility for their care and management. This includes providing the best diet possible. A good first step to providing this diet is to research the subject and discover what is the best diet for your Zebra Finch. The next logical step is to offer this new diet in such a way that the birds will eat it and enjoy it.

Just because your bird is eating the diet you are offering and appears healthy does not necessarily mean that you are feeding it the best diet possible. It does not even mean that your Zebra Finch is completely healthy. A well thought-out plan to alter the diet based upon the latest scientific research may produce a better nutritional balance, which in turn may produce a healthier bird who lives a longer life.

Feeding Companion Birds

Clearly, we still do not know enough about the natural (wild) diet of many cage and aviary birds. Of course, it is difficult, if not impossible, to allow captive birds to forage for their own food. Under ideal circumstances in the wild, birds know instinctively what to eat in order to satisfy their own particular nutritional requirements. This is not possible in captivity so it becomes all the more important that we learn how to feed our birds correctly.

Although most parrots, parakeets and finches do consume seeds, especially at certain times of the year, captive birds cannot live on seeds or pellets alone. In the wild, birds have the opportunity to seek out various fruits, leaves, buds, flowers, seeds, grasses, roots, bulbs, bark, insects and special calcium sources. It is our responsibility to offer the same type of variety to them in captivity.

A monotonous diet is stressful and boring to birds, and will result in restlessness, stress, feather plucking and unsatisfactory breeding. A balanced diet will contain a variety of ingredients, such as pellets/crumbles, seeds, vegetables, fruits and crushed nuts in appropriate qualities in order to maintain the captive birds in the best physical and emotional health.

Factors Affecting Nutritional Needs

A bird's food requirements are determined by its physiological conditions, its activity level and the demands of its habitat. Growth, breeding, egg-laying, rearing young, molting and the stress of daily life all increase a bird's nutritional requirements.

Other factors which influence the diet must also be seriously considered. In cooler climates for example, it would be necessary to have more fats and high-energy foods in the diet in order to maintain proper body temperature. The proper foods play an important role in acclimating the bird to these environmental conditions.

An adult, non-breeding bird that is very active requires more energy, and this energy comes from the diet. The number of hours of sunlight will also influence the bird's behavior and food requirements; the longer the days, the more activity and the need for more energy.

When molting, birds lose more body heat so they require more energy. In addition, they require larger amounts of proteins, especially lysine, to replace feathers.

Birds that are involved in breeding activities require more fats in the diet to create reserve energy supplies. During brooding, when birds remain in the nests for extended periods of time, these reserve fats ensure a constant body temperature. Hens also require extra nutrients, such as calcium, when producing eggs.

Seed

Zebra Finches are principally seed eaters, which means they feed on all types of grass and weed seeds available in their native habitat. In captivity, finches in general and domesticated species in particular, adapt easily to various kinds of millet—small-grained millet for all tropical and subtropical finches and somewhat larger-grained millet, like white millet, for the larger species such as Diamond Finches. All finches like canary grass seed or, as it is often called, white seed.

Millet spray, which is small-grained millet on the stalk, provides very important nutrients for birds. Scatter a few "ears" or "spikes" of millet spray so the birds can peck at them from all sides. My birds are never without millet spray; they love it and it is great fun for them as well!

This young Zebra Finch will need a more protein-intensive diet while it's growing.

Many Zebra Finches enjoy niger seed, rape seed and lin seed, which are rich in minerals. However, they also are high in fat and should be offered only in small quantities. Excessive consumption can cause liver problems.

Brown rice, which is included in some ready-made commercial bird seed mixtures, is suitable for Zebra Finches and the larger Australian finches, as well as some Lonchura species and other finches with strong beaks. However, it can lead to death in some birds, such as the Pin-tailed Parrot Finch (*Erythrura prasina*).

Soaked kernels of wheat and oats are much better additions to the basic food given to strong-beaked finches, like Zebra Finches. These soaked grains

*Offer your Zebra
Finch a variety
of seeds for a
healthy diet.*

may constitute as much as two-thirds of the total
amount of sprouted food. However, finches, especially
Diamond Finches, in cramped quarters grow fat easily
on oats!

All seed should be clean, dry, free of dust and of good
quality to prevent birds from ingesting harmful germs.
Various excellent seed mixtures are available on the
market. Always check the date of packing; do not buy
packages that are more than six months old.

SPROUTED SEED

In addition to dry food (seeds, pellets), Zebra Finches
need sprouted seeds. During the winter, these substi-
tute for green foods and immature seeds. They contain
valuable nutrients, including vitamin E, which is particularly important during the mating season.

There are various ways to produce sprouts, but a fresh
batch must be started every day. Here are two tested
methods for sprouting seeds:

- Mix 2 parts small-grained millet (panicum millet,
  for example) and 1 part canary grass seed in a
  large pot. Add water to soak so the seeds will swell.
  To speed up the process, place the pot on a radiator or in a warm room. Place the seeds in a sieve
  and rinse thoroughly under running water two or
  three times a day. Return them to the pot with
  fresh water. After 24 hours, the seeds are ready for

use. Dry them lightly with a clean towel, then mix in a few drops of cod-liver oil. This helps the sprouts remain moist longer, adds to their nutritional value and supplies vitamin D.

- Mix two-thirds small-grained millet, a little large-grained millet and no more than one-fourth canary grass seed in a pot. Add water to soak so the seeds can swell and leave them for 12 hours. Place the seeds in a sieve and rinse thoroughly under running water. Return them to the pot, cover it and let it sit for another 24 hours. The seeds then may be fed to the birds.

The choice of seeds to be sprouted depends, of course, on the tastes of your birds. Exotic finches from Africa, for example, like small-grained millet and canary grass seed, while those from Australia also enjoy soaked large-grained millet and other seeds, like nigerseed and rapeseed.

Spikes of millet can be sprouted as described above, but it is extremely important to change the water frequently so the cores of the spikes will not rot. Discard the water after 24 hours and set the spikes upright in a glass. Let the glass stand on a radiator for another day until the sprouts become visible. The sprouts then may be fed to the birds.

Millet also may be sown in small flower pots or saucers. After a few days, pots containing sprouted millet may be placed in the cage or aviary. Zebra Finches enjoy eating the young, 1-inch tall plants. Don't provide more sprouted seed than the birds can eat in a single day. Remove any leftovers in the evening because soured seeds can cause intestinal problems.

Pellets

In recent years, serious attempts have been made to improve the standards of the companion bird diet. Until recently, studies on pet nutrition were very limited because few companies had the manpower and the financial resources necessary to do such research. However, during the mid-1980s and 1990s ambitious research programs were implemented and completed by private parties and commercial bird feed manufacturers at various American, Canadian and European universities. Questions pertaining to the nutritional requirements of pet and aviary birds were examined in depth. The consequence of these studies was the development of a wide variety of nutritionally formulated bird pellets and crumbles. Some of these products were even geared towards specific bird groups (for instance, specific pellets for finches and canaries, specific pellets for parakeets, for small parrots, for macaws and large conures, and so on).

THE BENEFITS OF PELLETS

1. A good pellet/crumble improves avian health, growth and reproduction.

2. Pellets and crumbles reduce incidence of disease and stress because of their nutritional benefits.

3. A good-quality complete pellet will contain all the necessary components (proteins, carbohydrates, fats, vitamins, minerals).

4. *Lactobacillus acidophilus* is often added to the pellet mixture. This is a naturally occurring group of beneficial organisms that may help to maintain an optimal intestinal pH. It will not prevent disease, but it will strengthen the immune system and help to reduce the possibilities of introduction of disease.

5. Yucca is another common additive. This plant-extract decreases odors from manure and urine gas production.

6. Most commercial pellets and crumbles are economical to feed, and there is minimal waste. As an added benefit, there are no seed hulls to clean up.

7. One can target the needs for particular birds in specific situations because of the availability of the two general types of pelleted diets: breeder and maintenance.

8. Most commercial brands have been used and tested for a number of years under varying environmental conditions, demonstrating their effectiveness for all phases of a pet bird's life cycle. They also have been shown to be both palatable and nutritionally sound.

A good quality pellet contains all the nutrients your Zebra Finch needs for a healthy diet, though a pelleted diet should still be supplemented with fruits and vegetables.

Most commercial pelleted diets are nutritionally balanced and designed to be fed as a major part of the diet. However, do remember that reasonable portions of fresh vegetables and fruits as well as fun treats and a variety of birdseeds and such should be offered daily.

SWITCHING FROM A SEED-BASED TO A PELLET-BASED DIET

Sometimes converting your bird to a pelleted diet can be a difficult thing. Birds want to eat what they are familiar with, and introducing new foods can sometimes present a challenge.

We must offer birds foods that produce life sustaining energy in sufficient amounts to insure optimal health and well being. We must also make sure the foods are appealing enough that they are actually consumed. One could create a perfect avian pellet, but if it is not eaten it is doing little good.

Habit plays an important role in a bird's choice of food. Simply put, they like to eat what is familiar.

Therefore, any alteration of a bird's diet should be made very gradually. Birds recognize foods by their appearance. If birds receive pelleted food in place of a seed mixture, the actual size of the pellets will play a major role in its acceptability to them.

Since it is often rather difficult to cajole certain birds to switch from seed mixtures to pelleted foods, great patience, care and understanding must be exercised.

When first initiating your Zebra Finches and other birds to a pelleted diet, try blending the pellets with the familiar diet. Using the example of seeds, blend the pellets with the seeds and gradually reduce the seed diet and increase the pellets over a period of approximately 16 days. This tried and tested method is as follows:

Day 1–4: 25 percent pellets/
crumbles and 75 percent current seed mix.

Day 5–10: 50 percent pellets/
crumbles and 50 percent current seed mix.

Day 11–15: 75 percent pellets/crumbles and
25 percent current seed mix.

Day 16: 100 percent pellets/
crumbles.

Another trick is to moisten the pellets with fruit juice (apple or orange), and this sweetness and fruit flavor may help to make the pellets more palatable. (Remember that because of the possible growth of bacteria, wet food should be removed after 4 hours and replaced with clean, dry food.) Ideally, after 16 days the birds should be completely converted to the pelleted diet. If you are experiencing difficulty with your birds and were not successful on the first attempt, begin at step one and repeat the process. Sometimes it may take several attempts to successfully convert your birds to pellets.

Keep in mind that once a bird begins to eat a colored pelleted diet (the colors are created by the vegetable dyes), the droppings will also change colors, which is usually a brownish-red color. Droppings may become somewhat looser due to the extra trips to the drinking dish while eating the rather dry pelleted food. However, we do not want to see "watery" droppings.

Green Foods

Zebra Finches should receive an abundance of fresh green food. Possible foods to offer are chickweed, collard, leaf and bibb lettuce, endive, spinach, cabbage, pieces of carrots and carrot tops, celery leaves, broccoli and dandelion.

Fresh greens may be found in meadows and fields and along country lanes. However, plants growing alongside busy roads will be contaminated by exhaust fumes. Owners who lack a sure source of organic greens should grow them themselves.

In the case of English rye grass, wild millet and annual panicled grasses (except dandelions), give finches the entire head along with the stem. With dandelions, pick off the top of the plant after all the yellow petals have

> **SAMPLE ZEBRA FINCH MENU**
>
> Daily Seed Mixture:
>
> Millet (equal proportions of red, white, yellow etc.)—40 percent
> Canary Grass seed—35 percent
> Flax—5 percent
> Poppy—5 percent
> Hulled Oats or Rapeseed—10 percent
> Oat Groat—5 percent
>
> Daily Extras (in small amounts):
>
> Apple (raw)
> Spinach
> Bread (stale, milk- or water-soaked)
> Sunflower seeds (cracked)
> Cracker meal
> Weed seeds
> Peanuts (cracked)
> Wheat germ

fallen off. Give finches the entire chickweed plant; they eat the seeds and also pick at the leaves.

In addition, home-grown millet is very popular with Zebra Finches and other exotic finches. The ears should be harvested in the fall when they are partially ripe.

Fruit

Zebra Finches love to nibble on pieces of apple, pears, bananas, tomatoes, oranges, melons, cherries, grapes, grapefruit, berries, raisins and currants (the latter two also may be given soaked). Big pieces of fruit should be provided on feeding spikes, such as nails hammered into a board, so they will stay clean. Greens and fruit also can be provided in wire baskets sold commercially for this purpose.

Food of Animal Origin

Practically all exotic finches, including Zebras, like to eat food of animal origin: insects such as termites, ant pupae (ant eggs), small spiders and similar material, as well as man-made substitutes such as egg food, rearing food, etc. Such food becomes a necessity during the breeding season.

The amount of animal protein needed on a daily basis or when young are being raised varies considerably among different species. (Thin-beaked finches, particularly those from Africa, require much more animal food than birds with heavy beaks, like Zebra Finches.)

Eggs are the cheapest source of animal protein, and various excellent commercial products are on the

---

NUTRITIOUS TREATS

Offer your Zebra Finch some of the following nutritious treats several times a week:

Spinach
Romaine lettuce
Celery leaves
Broccoli
Carrot tops
Dandelions
Millet sprays
Chickweed
Apples
Grapes
Tomatoes
Bananas

And get creative in offering the food as well. Try placing pieces of fruit on spikes inside the cage. offer millet and other grasses upright in a container filled with wet sand; hang vegetables from the side of the cage. Offering a variety of food in a variety of ways will help you keep your finches interested in their food and prevent boredom.

market. Mealworms, the larval form of the darkling beetle, are another source of animal protein. However, Zebra Finches will only rarely eat live mealworms, even when the larvae are quite small. They prefer chopped and freshly scaled or just-hatched mealworms. They do not eat the entire larvae; they merely suck out the inside and leave the empty shell.

You can easily gather an insect treat for your Zebra Finches with a small net.

A good menu includes moths, fly larvae and enchytrea (white worms), with occasional substitution of tubifex, red mosquito larvae and water fleas (daphnia) for variety. These are best bought commercially. A good pelleted diet can be satisfactorily enriched with finely diced boiled egg and small insects.

Vitamins, Minerals and Trace Elements

Zebra Finches living free in their native habitats select from a great variety of insects, seeds and fruits to complete their diets. It is difficult for us to duplicate these dietary elements, hard as we might try. This lack of dietary variety can lead to vitamin deficiencies among captive birds. Fortunately, many commercial multivitamins are available as supplements to these birds' normal diets.

Zebra Finches also need to have access to supplements with minerals and trace elements, which are essential for proper plumage, good bone structure and healthy internal organs. These elements are present in finely ground boiled egg shell (commercially available) and oyster shell, cuttlebone, enriched limestone and commercial low-salt grit. However, the grit should not have a high charcoal content because some scientists believe charcoal removes vitamin A, B2 and K from the intestinal tract and contributes to vitamin deficiency.

Drinking Water

Most bird fanciers use water bottles with stainless steel drinking tubes or earthenware dishes. The latter solution, however, isn't very hygienic because Zebra Finches bathe in their drinking water. Small water fonts and automatic waterers don't get dirty and, of course, birds can't bathe in them.

Check the water supply at least once a day, more often (several times per day!) during hot summer weather. Bathing dishes get dirty rather quickly and must be cleaned regularly.

For a special treat, dissolve some honey or grape sugar (glucose) in the birds' drinking water a few times per week. Occasionally, give them a small dish of fruit juice. Cover these dishes with wire netting so birds won't bathe in them.

If your water is highly chlorinated, supply rain water instead of tap water. Boil it, then cool it for at least 3 hours before giving it to the birds. Spring water, available commercially in various brands, also is excellent.

Feeding Tips

Consistent and professional management practices are important to the success of the feeding and nutritional program.

Discard fresh foods and particularly cooked foods daily or even more often if they are not consumed. This is especially important in hot climates or where the ambient temperatures are likely to make foods spoil more quickly.

Keep food fresh by cleaning and replenishing the feeders daily. Some foods, such as pellets and/or seeds, should be available at all times. Clean feeders at least every other day to prevent mold and refill with fresh food. Keep water bottles and automatic watering systems clean and always have fresh water available in a constant supply. Store all commercial seed, pellets and crumbles in a cool, dry place to maintain maximum nutritional value.

Use feeding time as an opportunity to examine and observe your birds.

Nothing is as important as getting Zebra Finches accustomed to a fixed daily routine. Furnish drinking water, bath water and food at the same time each day. Soft food can be furnished with the regular morning food. This way, the finches can consume it as needed, especially if any nestlings must be fed. It also minimizes chances of spoilage. Remember to remove any leftover perishable food from the cage or aviary each evening (again, at a regular time).

Provide seed in open dishes (with a lip) or automatic feeders. Before adding fresh seed, blow away empty hulls. If using automatic feeders, remember to check that the seed flow isn't jammed.

Wash out the dishes every time you provide fresh bathing and drinking water. As you perform these chores, softly whistle a tune or talk quietly to the birds to keep them calm. A regular routine—regular whistling or humming, regular clothes, regular chore time—helps the birds become accustomed to your presence. Consequently, they will not become upset even if you need to look into the nest during the breeding season or when you perform chores near them while they are brooding or feeding their young.

Take the opportunity to individually examine birds in the collection. Lay each bird on its back in the palm of your hand and then blow aside some breast and stomach feathers so you can inspect the skin. The breast and stomach should have a healthy red color. The presence of any yellow discoloration generally indicates that the bird has grown too fat on too many oil-rich seeds. This situation can be corrected by adjusting the bird's diet gradually and by housing it in a facility where it has more room to exercise.

Your Zebra Finch's

Health

This book will help you learn what your bird should eat, how it should live and how it reproduces. But what makes it all work? Your bird's body is the key. It may seem that you have little in common physically with your birds, but in fact, you and your bird share  the majority of your biological systems. You have digestive, respiratory, skeletal, excretory and nervous systems that are very similar. Of course, there are some obvious and important differences.

Anatomy of a Zebra Finch

Knowing more about how your bird's body works will enable you to understand your feathered friend better; learning about the different parts of your bird's anatomy will enable you, in a medical emergency, to describe your bird's symptoms more clearly to the vet and to understand what the vet is saying.

One of the most obvious differences between your body and your finch's (apart from size!) is that your finch's body is adapted for flight. Although obvious expressions of this adaptation are your finch's wings and streamlined body shape, there are numerous internal structures that have adapted to flight as well.

If you notice that one of your finches is looking ill, remove it from the other birds immediately and place it in a hospital cage.

SKELETAL SYSTEM

A bird's skeleton is one of the structures that has developed for flight. Like us, birds have two legs, but the front limbs have evolved into bones that form the wings. And, did you know that some bird bones are hollow? These hollow bones (called pneumatic bones) make the bird lighter and flying easier, but also mean a bird's bones are fragile. Be careful when you are handling your bird! Its bones can snap and break with very little pressure.

Other skeletal adaptations for flight include a strong, enlarged breastbone (sternum) and strong pectoral muscles. These well developed muscles attach to the large sternum, giving the bird the muscle power and skeletal support it needs to fly.

Feathers

Although feathers are not part of your bird's skeletal system (they are in fact composed of the same material as your hair and fingernails), they are such an important structure that they bear closer investigation.

One reason people are so fascinated by birds is their ability to fly. Although the bird's whole body is uniquely adapted to flight, the feather is the most outwardly beautiful and symbolic of these adaptations. Birds' ancestors were reptiles, and feathers actually evolved from reptiles' scales.

The long feathers on the wings and tail are called **flight feathers;** the smaller feathers that cover the body and wings are known as **contour feathers. Down feathers,** the small, fluffy feathers on the breast and under the other feathers, provide insulation and warmth. In addition to enabling the bird to fly, feathers provide protection and warmth, and the coloration of the feathers is used for both camouflage and sexual display.

RESPIRATORY SYSTEM

Like all living things, both you and your Zebra Finch need oxygen to survive, and like you, your Zebra Finch has lungs filled with blood vessels that transfer oxygen to and from the air that is breathed in. However, your Zebra Finch's respiratory system works slightly differently from a human's. Air enters your finch's respiratory system through the **nares,** and then passes into the throat. From there it travels into the **choana,** the slit that can be seen easily in the roof of your bird's mouth, where it is warmed and moistened.

Then the air passes over the **syrinx,** the voice box, and on into the **lungs.** However, your bird's lungs don't expand and contract to draw the air in, as your lungs do. Instead, your bird's body wall expands, drawing the air in. To expirate, the body wall tightens around the lungs, forcing the air out.

A bird's body is very efficient at exchanging gases, but two complete breaths are required for the same work that one breath accomplishes in humans. You will notice that your bird appears to be breathing very fast—it is!

CARDIOVASCULAR SYSTEM

The cardiovascular system functions to carry necessary elements through the body, including oxygen, hormones, nutrients and other chemicals. Like the human heart, your finch's heart is four-chambered, with two **atria** and two **ventricles.** The heart pumps the blood, which carries the necessary nutrients, through the body.

One thing to keep in mind about your bird concerns blood quantity. Because your bird is so small, even the loss of a few drops of blood can be life threatening. Any bleeding must be controlled immediately!

DIGESTIVE SYSTEM

A bird's energy requirements are very high, and in fact, your bird may need to eat about 20 percent of its body weight daily to keep up with its energy needs. For this reason, both the respiratory and digestive systems must be very efficient.

The digestive system begins with the **beak.** The shape of a bird's beak is determined by the kind of food it eats. Raptors, like hawks, have sharply hooked beaks that enable then to catch and tear into their prey. Your Zebra Finch has a symmetrical beak in which the top (the upper mandible) part meets up neatly with the lower beak (the lower mandible). This shape of beak is effective for pecking and gathering seeds, your finch's main food in the wild.

Of course, birds have no teeth. This is another flight adaptation: No teeth means less weight in the head, and a lighter load to carry through the air. Since birds have no teeth, they must break down their food through other means. After your bird puts a seed in its mouth, the food moves into the **esophagus,** where it is moistened, and then into the **crop,** where it is further moistened and broken down.

From there the food enters the stomach, or at least the first stomach, the **proventriculus,** where digestive juices are added. The food then passes into the

gizzard, where it is ground into still smaller pieces, then into the **small intestine,** where more digestive juices are added and nutrients are absorbed into the blood stream. The unused portion of the food is then passed into the **large intestine,** then the **cloaca,** and is finally eliminated through the **vent.**

Birds can only store small amounts of waste materials, and your bird will eliminate frequently. This is why birds, unlike other animals, produce small amounts of droppings often.

The kidneys create urine which is also released through the vent along with the unused food. Bird urine is part liquid and part solid; the white material you see in your bird's droppings is uric acid. The urine passes from the **kidneys,** through the **ureter** and into the cloaca and out the vent. Unlike humans and other mammals, birds do not have a bladder or urethra.

NERVOUS SYSTEM

Your finch's nervous system is very similar to your own. It is made up of thousands of nerves that carry the messages from the body's sensory organs through the spinal cord and up to the brain. So what kind of messages is your finch's body receiving? How does your finch perceive the world around it?

YOUR BIRD'S SENSES

Smell and Taste   Because birds are adapted to flight and spend so much time in the air and off the ground, their sense of smell and the related sense of taste are poorly developed. Odor is most intense closest to its source and dissipates quickly in the air.

Hearing   Birds do have ears, although you can't see the ear opening without close investigation. They do not have ear flaps (pinnae) like humans or dogs; instead the ears are hidden under feathers. The lack of ear flaps and the close feather covering help to stream-line the bird in yet another adaptation to flight. Birds' ears are located on the sides of the head at the level of the lower beak. If you part the feathers you can see the small ear openings.

Sight Because birds spend much time in the air and in the trees searching for food on the ground below or far away, their eyesight is very keen. Birds' eyes are positioned on either side of the head, so their vision is monocular, meaning they use each eye independently. Although birds can't move their eyes around much, their necks are highly mobile. You will notice that your finch tilts its head when he wants to examine a particular object.

Touch Although parrots are more exploratory than their smaller finch relatives, the latter still picks up information about its environment from its feet, skin and beak. Finches' feet are evolved for life in the trees. One toe points backward and three point forward, enabling the bird to perch safely and effectively.

Birds' skin is thin and has no sweat glands. Like dogs, birds pant to cool themselves off. If you notice your bird holding his wings away from his body and panting with his mouth open, get him to a cooler place immediately!

YOUR AVIAN VETERINARIAN

Before you bring your Zebra Finch home, locate an avian vererinarian who will be able to offer advice and medical attentions should the need arise. Don't wait until there's an emergency before finding a good vet for your bird! Ask for recommendations from your friends who have birds, from your local bird club or from the breeder from whom you purchased your bird. Make sure you visit the vet's office and are pleased with the vet and the facilities before you commit your Zebra Finch to his or her care.

Molting

At least once a year your bird will molt, or lose its feathers. New feathers should grow in between 6 and 8 weeks. However, because captive birds are generally kept in warm temperatures year-round, your Zebra Finch may undergo constant, though less severe, molting. Molting can be stressful for birds, particularly older ones, and you may want to offer a dietary supplement that includes calcium and protein.

The new feathers coming in are called pin feathers, which makes sense when you see the small pointed ends of the new feathers poking through the skin. When a feather first begins to grow in, it is surrounded by a keratin sheath; this sheath falls off or gets rubbed off by an itchy bird as the feather grows in. New feathers have a blood supply that runs through the shaft. When the feather is completely grown, the blood supply dries up.

Avian Ailments

Often the first sign that Zebra Finches are sick is listless behavior at the feeding station, where they drop more food than they eat. In most cases, you will also notice swollen or dull eyes and puffed-up feathers. Sick birds often look like pitiful balls of feathers cowering in a corner, sleeping with the head buried deeply in the feathers. They loose interest in their surroundings, they loose their appetite (anorexia) or persist in staying at the feeding cup (polyphagia). Breathing is likely to be rapid.

HOSPITAL CAGE

Your first action should be to remove the bird from the cage or aviary, and keep it separate in a heated hospital cage. Then consult an avian veterinarian immediately. Keep an eye on the droppings and collect some for examination by your vet. Droppings may change color and may be loose, probably because the patient is drinking more than normal.

Keep the Sick Bird Warm

Warmth is extremely helpful to recovery, so the patient should be placed in a hospital cage immediately. Such a cage is completely closed, except for the front, which has wire mesh. You even can cover the front with a glass panel or with a cloth, if that seems advisable. Put a dark, infrared lamp of 75, 150 or 250 watts at a distance of 12 to 18 inches (30 to 50 centimeters) from the hospital cage. Check with your hand to make sure that the inside of the cage isn't getting too hot.

The best temperature for the living space in the hospital cage is 104 degrees F (40 degrees C), with as little variation as possible. As soon as the sick bird gets better, the temperature can be dropped gradually. One or more hospital cages should be essential equipment for every dedicated aviculturist!

COMMON CONDITIONS

Bald spots   Feathers can drop out due to vitamin deficiencies, mite infections or calcium deficiency. To deal with the problem, make sure the rations are adequate. I suggest you add low-salt grit to the diet. Be sure that there is enough vitamin A, D and B. If there are mites, get a good miticide (ask your pet dealer for advice). Ask your avian veterinarian about adding antibiotics to the drinking water.

Broken legs   The legs of Zebra Finches are thin and quite vulnerable. A leg can break easily, especially during a mishap in the catching process. If you suspect this has happened, consult your avian veterinarian as soon as possible. If your vet is not available, you can try to splint the leg yourself.

Zebra finches' legs are thin and delicate, and can break easily. If you suspect this has happened to your bird, consult and avian veterinarian immediately.

First, capture the patient with the utmost care. Then splice the leg with a moderately thick feather shaft (like a chicken feather) or a plastic drinking straw cut lengthwise. Attach the splint with woolen yarn or surgical tape and then make it rigid with collodion, surgical glue or plaster of Paris. Be sure to remember not to wrap the broken leg too tightly. Put the patient in a small hospital cage. Cover the floor with a thick layer of sand. Place food and water on the floor so that the bird can reach it easily. Remove all perches. Provide extra supplements of limestone, cuttle bone and vitamin D. You can take off the splint after approximately twenty days by dissolving it in acetone; be extremely careful as the fumes may be harmful to the patient. If the leg hasn't turned black, you can assume that the operation was successful.

Broken wings   These are very difficult to correct. The best thing to do is consult an avian vet. Don't try a home treatment.

Constipation   Constipation frequently results from feeding too much egg food, especially if it is too dry. An excess of poppyseed may also cause problems. Other causes can be spoiled or old seed.

Birds with constipation puff up the feathers and stay perched or nervously run up and down. Sometimes it is clear that they can't relieve themselves. The rear of the body may even be swollen. They stop eating and act sluggish. Remedy the problem with green food, a lot of fruit and rape seed rubbed with fat. Add antibiotics to the drinking water and vitamins to the food. Above all, be sure that the food you furnish is top quality and fresh.

Egg binding   Egg binding is the condition in which the hen can't lay an egg that's ready to be laid. A major cause is breeding a female too young. Never breed female finches younger than one year or older than five years.

Other possible causes include breeding females that have gotten too fat or too weak or those that have a serious calcium deficiency. Cold, drafty sleeping quarters could also be a contributing factor. Finally, it is possible that the oviduct isn't developed properly or has become infected. If this last condition is at fault, there is little we can do about it; the only option is to not breed these females.

To help expel a "stuck" egg, gently dip the lower half of the female's body in alternately cold and luke-warm water. Dab some vegetable oil "under the tail" (in the vent). Put the patient in a hospital cage at 90 degrees F (32 degrees C); when the egg is laid, reduce the temperature slowly to normal. Whatever you do, don't take a chance on breaking the egg inside the bird's body, this could have fatal results. Add antibi-otics to the drinking water. If you have to artificially promote laying, be sure not to use the eggs produced this way for breeding. In all cases, consult an avian vet-erinarian immediately.

Egg pecking   Birds will peck at their own eggs or those of other exotic finches when we don't furnish enough cuttle bone, limestone, grit and vitamins dur-ing the year, but especially during the breeding season. Boredom can also be a cause. Be sure the supplements I just mentioned are in adequate supply, and provide extra vitamin A and D. Counteract boredom by using your imagination in varying the diet. Hang up some jute ropes or, once in awhile, a piece of raw red meat to attract their interest.

Eye infection   If a bird has an eye problem, for example excessive tearing, place the bird in a dark-ened cage and treat the infected eye with 5 percent boric acid ophthalmic ointment (Neosporin or Neopolycin), after first rinsing out the eye with luke-warm water or a 0.9 percent saline solution. Add vita-min A and D to the food. Eye infection is often caused by bacteria, so keep perches and housing clean.

Feather picking   Birds sometimes pick the feathers of another bird in more than an occasional way. This can be caused, for example, by boredom, stress, vita-min-, protein-, calcium- and other mineral deficiencies or overcrowding. Feather picking not to be confused with preening, which is bonding and beneficial; in feather picking the result is bald spots on the victim's body.

First of all, immediately improve the diet, especially the vitamin and mineral content, and add rearing and egg food to the diet, preferably year-round. Add antibiotics (ask your vet) to the drinking water. If you have too many birds in one cage, thin out the collection or buy more cages. Be sure to immediately remove any loose feathers that lie on the floor.

If, despite your countermeasures, the problem persists, a light spray with Bitter Apple (available in pet supply stores) may help. Be sure not to get any spray in the birds' eyes. Whatever you do, don't wait before you take action against feather picking.

Mite infestation   Red mites (*Dermanyssus avium*) are the worst. This blood-sucking arachnid surfaces from dark hideaways during the night. Favorite hiding places are cracks and seams (especially in nest boxes). In heavy infestations, mites may even stay on the birds during the day, so it isn't always good enough to transfer affected birds to another, uninfested facility, even if it is thoroughly disinfected. It also doesn't help to let an infested facility stand empty in hopes of getting rid of red mites; they can live without eating for at least 5 or 6 months!

A red mite infestation is easy to notice. The birds are restless at night and peck and scratch continuously. If you shine a flashlight at the birds or their perches, you will be able to see the red parasites easily in most cases. Take good care that you do not personally pick up any mites, because they can cause an irritating, burning eczema in humans; a heavy case can even cause anemia.

Mite infestation can be brought in by wild birds or new purchases and can progress rapidly. A single female mite can produce approximately 2,600 eggs in her lifetime so it pays to keep alert. During daylight, run a pocketknife through cracks and crevices. If you don't get any blood on it, then there's no trouble. Or else, lay a white cloth in the sleeping coop or on the cage and look for mites on the cloth the next morning.

The moment you confirm a mite infestation, remove all birds from the facility and spray it with a contact insecticide. (Ask your pet store manager to recommend a good product.) Some sprays now on the market can be used without removing birds from the facility. Be sure to spray all holes, crevices, joints, perches, wire mesh, nest boxes, food and water dishes (especially the sides and bottoms) and all other utensils and equipment in the facility. Remove all nesting material and burn it. After letting the insecticide work its benefits for several days, wash everything thoroughly with soapy water. Rinse cages with boiling water. Make sure that your storage areas are also free of mites, otherwise a new infestation will be launched from there. Treat your birds with a powder insecticide or with some commercial brand of spray. Be sure to follow label directions.

Use the same remedies for feather lice, feather mites and shaft mites. These species live on the carotene (protein) of the feather shaft, causing the feathers to drop and general growth and development to be stunted. I can't say enough that absolutely proper sanitation in the bird facility is the only lasting remedy.

Overheating When birds are overheated they show it! They will sit there with wings drooping and pant rapidly with the beak open. This is their way of trying to get cool as they do not have sweat glands in the skin like we do. Like dogs, they must rely on the moisture evaporating from the mucus membranes inside the mouth to help reduce temperature. Cool the bird off by spraying it with cool water or placing a fan in front of the cage. Contact your veterinarian.

Enjoying

Your

part three

Zebra
Finch

Breeding
Zebra Finches

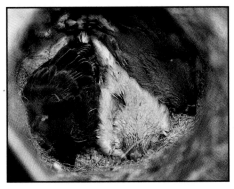

One of the things that most attracts people to Zebra Finches is the ease with which they breed in captivity. Even with Zebra Finches, however, breeding is not something that can be entered into blindly. Read this chapter thoroughly, and follow up with some of the books listed in chapter 11. Make sure your accommodations are clean and spacious, your birds are good, healthy specimens and you will be able to provide the best nutrition, as breeding can be taxing for your birds, especially for the female. You must also be sure that you will be able to comfortably keep the offspring that result or find good homes for all of them. When you decided to keep birds, you agreed to provide for all their needs; likewise, if you decide to breed, you must provide for the increased needs of your birds, and also for the health, well-being and needs of their offspring.

The care and breeding of Zebra Finches is not diffi-cult; beginners usually have greater success with Zebra Finches than with other species because the birds are not so demanding in their requirements and are very hardy. The birds will breed problem-free as long as you provide a variety of nest boxes and light, airy nest material that can be easily manipulated by the birds.

Zebra Finches should not be allowed to produce brood after brood just because they will do so. In such cases, the hen will only become exhausted and, sooner or later, this will affect the health of the youngsters.

Setting Up

Successful breeding depends on, among other things, healthy parents, good housing for the birds and proper food and supplements to keep the females strong. As the breeding season approaches, take some time to make sure your Zebra Finches' quarters are in top condition.

FRESH AIR

The importance of fresh air and sunlight should never be underestimated and this is important even in the winter months. Most breeders ventilate their cages and aviaries too little in the winter months as they are afraid it will be too cold for the birds. Zebra Finches and most other Australian finches are quite hardy and can withstand fairly low temperatures as long as they are well-fed and have instant access to shelter.

Closed shelters and cages pose problems if they are not adequately ventilated. Poor ventilation will soon lead to stale, bacteria laden air and a risk of disease, so birds should only be kept locked inside during very cold or inclement weather. It goes without saying that draft-proof sleeping boxes and a good, balanced diet should be provided. Many breeders will agree that, given the right conditions, fewer birds will be lost in the winter than during spring and fall.

Sunlight

Sunlight is also very important to all birds. It helps synthesize vitamins, kills bacteria and other potentially dangerous organisms and can be described as indispensable for our Zebra Finches. Ensure, therefore, that your indoor aviaries, birdrooms and night shelters are provided with large windows, facing south (in the northern hemisphere) if possible, to allow in maximum sunlight.

Cleanliness

At the beginning of the breeding season it is advisable to disinfect all nesting boxes before they are installed in the cages and aviaries. Of course, this is unnecessary if you are using new nest boxes. In general, Zebra Finches are extremely messy birds. The nest itself is kept relatively clean, but they press their droppings onto the sidewalls. With good ventilation this layer of droppings will dry out into a very hard "inner wall" and pose little or no danger to adults or youngsters. In badly ventilated nests, however, the nest becomes a smelly, wet mess and a source of infection.

Nest boxes should be cleaned out at the start of each breeding season, as Zebra Finches can be very messy birds!

Always keep your aviaries clean; remove droppings, seed husks, leaves and feathers regularly, and it is a good idea to hose the floor down periodically. Indoor walls of the aviary should be whitewashed or given a coat of good emulsion paint at least once a year.

How Many Pairs?

The finch fancier has since bought a good pair of Zebra Finches. With excitement, he takes the birds home and he has made the first step towards a hobby that will be a source of joy, and an interesting, expanding and useful pastime. There are some beginners with a larger purse who are perhaps tempted to start with two or more pairs. There is nothing wrong with this, but, the beginner can probably learn more of the basics from a single pair than he can with ten as, in the latter case, he lose his oversight all too quickly. It is also not a good idea to place too many birds together in a cage unless it is large enough for each pair to have its own territory. Even two pairs in a small cage will not produce good breeding results due to continuous squabbling, infertile eggs, restless brooders and bald plucked youngsters! Of course, quarreling will practically disappear altogether with several pairs in a large colony breeding aviary.

I have obtained my best breeding results either with a single pair in a good sized cage, or with three to five pairs in the colony breeding aviary. The amount of room available will of course decide how many pairs can be accommodated. Spread over three broods, we can often reckon on raising four to five youngsters per pair. These youngsters must be separated from the parents when the adults wish to start on the next round of breeding and placed together in a large cage or aviary until they have their adult plumage. An ideal situation is to have three extra flights; one for growing up the young birds and the other two in which to separate the cocks and hens before they reach complete adulthood.

Remember Zebra Finches and the other Australian finches are very lively birds that require ample flying space. Breed with a fewer birds rather than overcrowd your available space.

Setting up Pairs

We must naturally keep our various color mutations separate if we do not want to end up with a jumble of homozygote (pure) and heterozygote (split) Zebra Finches. The birds should thus be kept color with color, for example gray with gray ("normals"), white with white, fawn with fawn, silverwing with silverwing and so on, if we are going to be serious about our color breeding.

The breeding pairs are best placed together at 1 year of age (although some are fertile and can produce eggs as early as $2^{1}/_{2}$ months).

RECORDS AND RECORDKEEPING

When you breed your Zebra Finches, it is of utmost importance for you to keep good records on the condition of your stock. Together with the use of leg bands, your records will help establish who's who in the aviary or breeding cages. You don't need anything fancy; a loose-leaf notebook will do the job.

Every bird should have its own page in your notebook. As time passes, the ensuing record will be of immeasurable value if you are a hobbyist who wants to accomplish something in the world of bird breeding. It will reflect your good management, which will make a favorable impression on any future purchaser.

It is of the greatest value that you maintain good breeding records. If you update them regularly, you will eventually be able to characterize your bird pairs as to traits they possess in visible or invisible form. You will be able to determine whether they breed well or poorly, eat heavily or sparingly, tend to fight or are peace loving and so on. It may take several breeding seasons before you know everything there is to know about your birds.

Let me show you an example of the records I keep by taking a page out of my own notebook on Zebra Finches. (In your own notebook, you can make any changes, improvements or additions that seem useful to you.)

Location: Breeding cage No. 75

I.D. No. of male: 55-1996

I.D. No. of female: 35-1996

Expressed coloration of male: Gray

Expressed coloration of female: Gray

Color of leg band (male and female): Blue

Notation: To differentiate them from any young they may produce, this pair of adult Zebra Finches have their colored leg bands on the right leg.

Birth date of Young: May 18, 1997

Leg bands of young: I.D. No.: 14-1997; 15-1997; 17-1997;18-1997 (No. 16-1997 died in an accident one week after fledging)

Coloration of Young:

14 (male): Gray (normal or wild color)

15 (male): Gray (same)

16 (male): Gray (deceased)

17 (female): Fawn

18 (female): Gray (normal or wild color)

Special Remarks:

1. Expressed coloration is that of normal gray Zebra Finches.
2. Not homozygous, as evident from coloration of young (gray and fawn).
3. Male parent bird passes down a fawn trait (No. 17 is a fawn female).
4. Female parent is an excellent breeder.

This record information forms the basis of a number of conclusions. Since fawn is a sex-linked trait, it seems from the breeding record that the male is not pure gray (or, technically, he is not homozygous); rather, he passes down a trait for fawn, as shown by the first brood in the fawn female, No. 17.

My conclusion regarding the fawn color trait was confirmed in the second round of breeding, which, according to my further records, produced two fawn females. If I now want to produce fawn males, I have to mate the male parent (No. 55) with one of his fawn daughters. This is an example of purposeful inbreeding. According to the rules of heredity, such a mating will produce fawn males as well, even if they don't appear in the first round of breeding. This cross also will produce fawn females and gray (normal) males, as well as females that are split for fawn. My intention is to produce the fawn males with which I will be able to breed homozygous fawn birds, ones that will inherit purely. If only for breeding purposes, keeping good records is of the utmost importance; in fact, you can't do without them.

You may also set up a card file—a good, but more time-consuming method of recordkeeping. Each bird gets its own card, which notes its description, vital information, events and the like. You can keep the cards in a ring binder or in a file box. An office supply store or printer can furnish blank perforated cards of any desired dimension or color. For a small fee, a printer can even cut cards to any specified size.

The file card can be set up in much the same way as the pages of a notebook. A typical card can record the following points, one beneath the other:

Color:

Date of Birth:

Color of Mother:

Ring No.:

Color of Father:

Ring No.:

Sex:

Ring No.:

Heredity Line:

Color of Grandmother:

Ring No.:

Color of Grandfather:

Ring No.:

Special Observation:

The more details you furnish on the file card, the better the information you will have on the bird involved and the more exact your breeding experiments will be. Also, when you are ready to sell the bird, proper records enable the buyer to have a complete picture from the wealth of detail you can provide.

A really well kept file card can sometimes reveal a surprisingly accurate picture of a bird. It indicates not only the genetic traits, but also such aspects as its behavior to birds of the same and other species and its breeding record. The record provides the means to differentiate birds of good quality from those of lesser quality. Good records will enable you to sell the really good birds to a true, enthusiastic breeder, reserving the other birds for the impulse buyer. It is also now possible to keep records of your Zebra Finches and other birds on a personal computer.

Colony Breeding

One disadvantage of breeding single pairs of Zebra Finches in cages is that breeding results are often somewhat less successful than those in a colony system. The reason for this is not easy to ascertain. A pair may not be particularly compatible, so the clutch, the incubation and the rearing of the young are not wholly successful. Sometimes it is necessary to break up an established pair of Zebra Finches to breed selectively for color. Both birds from the original pair may not readily accept a new "spouse," especially if the former spouse is still in sight or even in hearing range.

In a colony breeding aviary or cage, the selection of partners is left to the birds themselves. The cock will choose his own mate and this partnership will usually stay intact with little or no objection from the other birds in the colony. In fact, colony breeding encourages birds to stay "true" to each other for life! In such cases, breeding results are likely to be consistently more successful than those from "forced" pairings.

An experiment to compare six single Zebra Finch pairs breedings and six further pairs in colony breeding produced the following results:

	Clutch 1	Clutch 2	Clutch 3
Single Pairs:	17	15	16
Colony Pairs:	19	27	22

The single pairs lost in this case, 48 to 68! It would be premature to come to a concrete conclusion using these results. A much greater number of experiments would have to be carried out before we can make the statement that colony breeding gives better results than single pair breeding. It can be said that, for example, colony breeding is more natural for Zebra Finches, as in the wild they tend to live and nest together in groups. However, it is interesting to note in the above results that the single pairs produced more regular figures.

One can quite easily breed selectively with the colony system by keeping birds of only one variety together in each cage or aviary. For example, a battery of three aviaries could contain respectively normal (gray), white and fawn Zebras. By selectively removing and introducing new blood, excellent lines can be produced.

It is also interesting to know that most Australian finches can be kept together in a mixed community with canaries or with many other small tropical birds such as: Society Finches, Silverbills, Firefinches, Golden-breasted Waxbills, Mozambique Siskins or Green Singing Finches, Red Avadavats, Orange-cheeked Waxbills, Red-tailed Lavender Finches, Bronze-winged Mannikins, Golden Song Sparrows, Cuban Finches or Cuban Grass Quits, Red-cheeked Cordon Blues, Diamond Doves and so on. A pair of

Zebra Finches can also be kept safely together with a pair of budgerigars (parakeets) or cockatiels, or a pair of flightless or pinioned quail. Bullies will have no chance in doing any harm to the fast-flying adult Zebra Finch, though one should keep watch on newly fledged youngsters if you have quail in the cage or aviary.

Banding is an easy way to identify your birds, facilitating record keeping and proper pairing for breeding.

Cage Breeding

Anyone wanting to keep strict breeding records has no choice but to breed his birds one pair per cage; it is the only way to know which youngsters come from which parents. It is also the only way to breed further with purebred birds and the only way to get first class exhibition stock. In colony breeding, any cock bird could be the father of a particular youngster! With colony breeding you cannot influence quality other than selection of the youngsters and you can, for instance, never be sure that any bird is not split for another color. In such cases unexpected colors often turn up inopportunely.

If you have a bird with a special color or pattern, you can only be sure to pass on or improve the same color or pattern by selective breeding with a single pair per cage. This is the only way the breeder can select the right partner for the right job. Anyone buying a new color mutation and introducing it to a colony aviary will find, ironically, that it will usually pair up with the "wrong" partner; not the one you had hoped! In such cases a color mutation can disappear in a generation or two. Anyone having the luck to accidentally breed a brand new mutation in his stock can best perpetuate the mutation by selective partnering with one of its own parents, and this, of course can only be done if the pair is housed separately. With colony breeding it will be almost impossible to find the right parent! It may be true that colony breeding is more likely to turn up a new mutation, but it is also the best means of losing it! There are even more advantages of breeding one pair per cage: Management is easier, and so is selection, while faults can be corrected by changing partners.

Another advantage of the system is that it is possible to have a better control of the diet. Birds that feed their young inadequately should not be allowed to start a second brood. However, a month or so's rest may solve the problem.

A good breeding cage (various models are readily available in the better pet supply stores, but you may be able to construct them yourself, as ready-to-use mesh fronts in different sizes are also available) must meet the demands of its purpose. It must not be too small as the birds must have enough room to fly; a good size is 24 × 16 × 16 inches. During construction try to avoid leaving any cracks and crannies that could harbor parasites. Glue and pin the sheets together and fill any holes or cracks with a good wood filler. The inside of the cage should be thoroughly sanded to remove any splinters, then painted with white undercoat followed by a good coat of white or light colored matte paint. It goes without saying that lead-free paint should be used. The smooth painted cage interior will minimize wear and tear on the birds' plumage and will give an altogether better view of the birds. Moreover, a painted cage is easy to clean with a wet cloth, and it is always easy to add another coat of paint when required.

A good practical method is to have a battery of identical cages that can be slid in and out of a stand like drawers. A dirty cage can then easily be removed and replaced by a clean one. Change the birds to the new cage and you can take the dirty cage somewhere else to be cleaned without any inconvenience to the birds. Such a system may be more costly, but it will pay for itself in saved time and trouble, and stress-free birds!

Cages should have room inside for two nest boxes. It is best to have all similar nest boxes, so changeovers do not worry the birds so much, and cleaning is made easier. The second nest box is often used by the young as a sleeping nest since Zebra Finches have a habit of starting on the next brood before the current one is independent. Having only one nest can lead to broken eggs or eggs being thrown out, and to the parents chasing the older youngsters out of the nest. A second nesting box in the cage will usually avoid these problems.

The entrance hole of the nest boxes should always face the center of the cage, not the front of the cage as is usually the case. The birds will then feel more secure because they can not see you directly out of the nest each time you enter the room.

Nest Boxes

In the wild, we know that Zebra Finches and other Australian finches construct domed nests from grass and twigs, lined with softer material. Theoretically, the best breeding results can be expected if the birds are allowed, as far as possible, to follow their instincts and make their own choice of nesting site. In such a case, plant a few conifers or other thickly foliaged shrubs in the aviary. A pile of hay and other nesting material is placed in one of the shelters, and the rest is left up to the birds. Some breeders are concerned only with the results and are not fussy about how the birds breed. For other breeders, the whole breeding process is regarded as one of the most interesting parts of the hobby. They would prefer not to miss a single detail and, if it were possible, some of these would like to keep their birds in transparent aviaries with transparent nest boxes! For these eager aviculturalists, therefore, nest boxes are best, as these allows them to check the nests, eggs and youngsters at regular intervals. Most Zebra

Finches have no difficulties with this, especially once they have become accustomed to their owners.

There is no proof that either of these breeding methods produce more offspring, however. One must obviously offer the most suitable kinds of nest boxes for the birds. This means that in particular aviaries or in particular climatic conditions, particular nest boxes are required.

There are many different kinds of nest boxes available for your Zebra Finches.

TYPES OF NEST BOXES

There are many kinds of nest boxes and the fourteen types described here could easily have been twenty! Almost every finch breeder eventually has his or her own design of nest box and is always convinced his or her box is the best! If you have not selected your favorite model then you are certain to find one you like from the following list:

1. Nest log: made from a length of hollowed-out birch trunk or limb with a screwed-on wooden lid. Very useful, warm sleeping accommodation for winter. Too warm in summer for indoor cages, and as breeding place in states with a hot climate (Florida, California, for example).

2. Nest box: constructed from $1/2$-inch ply or blockboard. Height 5 inches, length 4 inches, width 4 inches (approximately $12 \times 10 \times 10$ centimeters). The entrance hole is high on the front. Diameter $1^3/_4$ inches (3.5 cm). The lid turns on a screw. Ideal

warm sleeping box for the winter. A few small holes bored in the sides will aid ventilation. Not recommended as a breeding box during the summer months.

3. Nest basket: of woven raffia, straw or wicker. Warm, but well ventilated. Highly recommended. Easy to clean by immersing in boiling water.

4. Globular nest basket: made from plaited and woven hay. Warm and porous. Very good for both sleeping or breeding nests. Less easy to clean. A similar nest can be made from thick string and can be cleaned by immersing in boiling water.

5. Coconut nest box: a warm sleeping nest but less suitable for a breeding nest. Easy to clean.

6. Nest basket: made from so called "mouse mesh" or similar small gauge wire mesh. The shape is very close to the natural nest shape. Very suitable for either a sleeping or breeding nest. Adequate nesting material must be provided. Very easy to keep clean.

7. Plant pot nest: The drainage hole is enlarged to $1^3/_4$ inches (3.5 cm) with a drill. Very suitable for a sleeping or breeding nest. Warm in the winter; cool and porous in the summer. Easy to clean.

8. Wooden nest box: with large (half end) opening. Side walls supplied with ventilation holes. Can be cleaned by immersing in boiling water and thereafter painting the interior with whitewash or nontoxic paint. An ideal breeding box often selected by Zebra Finches.

9. Bunch of heather: Very simple and useful. Gives birds opportunity to build own nest from "scratch." Can be destroyed by burning after use.

10. Wooden nest box: roofed with plainted rushes or similar. Mesh can also be used. Floor dimensions 4 × 4 inches. Ideal breeding facility!

11. The "3 in 1"–model or three-pair nest box: with entrance holes in the center and at either end so that the breeding pairs do not need to squabble too much. Length 11.8 inches (30 cm). Very

suitable as a dormitory in winter. Clean by immersion in boiling water and paint interior with whitewash or similar.

12. Wooden nest box: with mesh sides, can be used winter or summer.

13. Cylindrical mesh nest: with half-round wooden half front and round back. Good breeding nest.

14. Flower pot nest: with half base removed. Very useful (see number 7).

It can be generally stated that a suitable sleeping nest box should not be too open, whereas a breeding nest should be adequately ventilated so bird droppings dry out as quickly as possible. To clean the nestboxes, immerse in boiling water and leave to soak for a few minutes so all bacteria, lice and other pests are killed. Use whitewash mixed with Lysol for a good hygienic coating of the interior. While you are cleaning one nestbox it is preferable to replace it with another of the same type so the birds will readily accept the new one and there will be minimal disruption.

Nest boxes should be installed as high up as possible in the cage or aviary, and they should be separated as far as possible from each other. This will minimize squabbling and help successful breeding.

Nest Material

As the breeding season approaches, adequate nesting material must be made available for your Zebra Finches. It would be impossible to list every item of material a Zebra Finch would use to construct its nest because it will use anything suitable that you offer it. Hay, straw, twigs, leaves, left-over green food, empty millet sprays, and pieces of rag or paper are just some of the items a Zebra Finch may use to construct its nest.

Most breeders, however, like to give special nest material, so the birds can construct a sound and tidy nest. Hay and unraveled sisal string is good (the hay first so it is used for the base of the nest). The nest will then be lined with the softer fibers, plus any feathers that can be found. When using string, clip it to maximum lengths of $2^1/_2$ inches before unraveling. There is always the danger that birds could get caught up and injured if longer lengths are given.

Zebra Finches are incorrigible muddlers in their nests. Some birds (Diamand Doves, for example) are continually cleaning their nests, even saving up the overnight droppings ready for disposal in the morning. Canaries on the other hand, keep the nest hollow clean, but deposit the droppings on the rim of the nest, probably in a failed attempt to remove them altogether. Zebra Finches follow the same method as canaries but with even less success, so the droppings quickly form a wall inside and on top of the nest.

This is obviously not good for nest ventilation, and that's why mesh nest baskets are ideal and why it is best not to give nest materials that soon deteriorate into a sticky mess. Wadding, kapok or cotton, for example, are not suitable nest materials. Elastic nest material, such as hay and sisal, is good for ventilation. A well ventilated nest will allow the droppings to dry out quickly so there is less of a danger of infection than there would be in the case of a sticky, dirty nest.

The nesting drive of most Zebra Finches and other Australian finches is so strong that, as long as nesting material is available, they will be building or adding to their nest. It is therefore recommended that enough material is given only to build one nest and any remaining material be removed so the birds can get down to the more serious matter of their young without too many distractions.

Once the young are hatched it is wise to make the occasional bit of nest material available so the parents can make running repairs. Remember, hay may not be easily available in the early part of the year when the breeding season begins, so the conscientious breeder is advised to save some sheaves of grass from the previous season.

Breeding Season

The most exciting time for the breeder is when every-thing for the breeding season has been prepared: The birds have been paired up, the nest boxes have all been placed in position and all the bird owner has to do now is wait and see what happens. The experienced breeder will have seen that his birds were correctly paired up during the preceding winter. He will have recorded the specialties of his birds in his record book and will have decided, for example, that the hen with ring No. 38 should be paired up with cock No. 26 in the coming season. His acquired knowledge of finch genetics will decide how the birds are paired up. The birds are then simply placed together in a breed-ing cage.

The beginner with little knowledge of genetics, or the person who has no notes on the past histories of his birds will have to try another system until he gets him-self organized. All cocks and hens are placed together in a low cage. Next, one of the cocks is removed and carefully examined for condition, before being placed in a breeding cage. The color pattern is carefully assessed; the good and bad points noted. If, for exam-ple, the cock has an astoundingly clean-cut white breast and belly, then one should choose the hen with similar attributes to be his mate. This will help pass the attributes on to the offspring. After a year's breeding in this manner, the breeder will have arrived at some sort of system and will have the beginnings of some good lines of birds.

The breeder has done his work and now it is up to the birds. For the beginner as well as the experienced fancier, it is always a great joy to see the birds respond-ing to their partner. Some birds will begin work almost as soon as a nest box and nest materials are made available. The cock in particular will start making continual flights between the floor of the cage/aviary and the nest box. The hen inspects the work from time to time, arranges nest material to her desire and tidies up bits that may be sticking out. Excited with the task before him, the cock drives away any intruders—other finches that may get too close—and continually sings his "tin-trumpet" song to his spouse. This song is always performed when the cock is excited and, at the same time, he sits up straight and fluffs out the feathers on his crown. The hen may appear to be quite unconcerned by all this ceremony at first but she will have accepted his advances and will begin sleeping with him at night in the unfinished nest.

Nest building in captivity takes a while, but as the cock works with increasing ardor, the nest begins to take shape. If the cock is building in a nest box, the whole box will be stuffed with hay as high as the entrance hole, and the nest hollow will be lined with a soft bed of fibers and feathers. At this stage the pair is ready to mate and the cock springs excitedly onto the hen's back; the hen wiggles her tail quickly backwards and forwards, a sign for the cock that she is ready for pairing. He reaches his tail around under hers so that their vents come into apposition and pairing is completed. Such a pairing may take place several times, and soon the hen disappears into the nest in order to lay her first egg.

Incubation

The eggs of the Zebra Finch (and all other Australian finches) are pure white, which is usual for birds that nest in enclosed nests or hollows; camouflage is less necessary for these eggs than for eggs laid in open nests.

With the first clutch, four eggs is usually the maximum. In later clutches more eggs may be laid. Incubation is carried out largely by the hen, but the cock takes his turn sometimes and both birds stay in the nest at night. None of the Australian grass finches can be described as calm during the nesting period; they are continually adding to the nest—a piece of hay here, a feather there; feeding, squabbling and continually chasing "nosy" neighbors away.

The beginner may be somewhat anxious that all this activity will have a bad effect on the welfare of the clutch, but with Zebras this is all part and parcel of the breeding season.

During breeding season, Zebra Finch hens usually lay four or more white eggs.

If the eggs are inspected after about 7 days, one can see which are fertile by holding them up against the light—fertile eggs will be no longer transparent; however this is not recommended as it is easy to damage the brittle little eggs and there is hardly room for two human fingers to be pushed into the nest opening. The eggs could be removed with a plastic teaspoon but even this is not necessary. You can see if the eggs are fertile or not by just looking at them in the nest. Fertile eggs will be darker in color and bluish, in contrast to the infertile eggs which have a slightly transparent pink tinge. Once you have seen a fertile egg next to an infertile one it will become easy.

Zebra Finches are not overly concerned by nest inspections, especially when these are carried out by the person who usually feeds and waters them and is thus the person they are most familiar with. It is recommended that inspections are carried out at regular times so the birds become accustomed to them. Incubation time varies from $12^{1}/_{2}$–$14^{1}/_{2}$ days. Incubation time may be influenced by the ambient temperature outside, and earlier clutches often take longer when the outside temperature is lower. The young hatch in the order of the age of the eggs, so there can be a few days difference in age between the first and last hatched. This difference in age is not so obvious as the young grow, because the parents tend to feed the younger hatchlings with more food so they grow faster and soon catch up with their brothers and sisters. The youngest members of the clutch thus usually fledge not more than 1 or 2 days after the oldest. After hatching, the small bits of egg shells are usually eaten by the parent birds, the larger pieces carried away from the nest and dropped.

The Hatchlings

The hatchlings are helpless and sparsely downed at first, but soon little feathers appear all over the body, and one can see whether the youngsters will be, for example, brown, gray or white. When very small, the young beg for food without making a sound. With the beak wide open, the tongue, with its marked white papillae, is moved back and forth, and the light-colored marks or stripes inside the cheeks are designed to attract and guide the parents to the open beak and to stimulate their instincts to feed the young. The parents keep the young crops filled with amazing industry and these swell up to the size of a pea. The unhusked millet-seed that has been softened in the parents' crops, is easy to see through the thin walls of the youngsters' crops.

Although they are very small, the youngsters are amazingly hardy. They can withstand the cold much better than young canaries, but this is probably helped by the enclosed nest. Occasionally a youngster falls out of the nest (perhaps hooked in the claws of one of the parents flying quickly out of the nest after a scare), and although it may fall several feet to the ground and lay there for a while before being discovered, if it is picked up and replaced in the nest it will usually recover in no time at all. Even if it is numbed with cold, it will soon recover, especially if you hold it for a while in your warm hand before putting it back among its warm brothers and sisters.

*These little
Zebra Finches
are the rewards
of careful
breeding.*

About three weeks after hatching, the young are ready to leave the nest. They will have become quite noisy and the breeder who does not inspect the nest will know that there are young present from the noise they make.

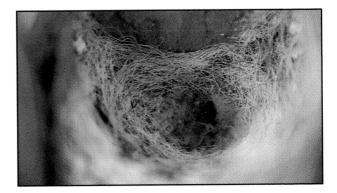

In the warmer months, especially, an underdeveloped youngster may leave the nest in an attempt to copy its brothers and sisters. In such cases the precocious youngster is best replaced in the nest. On leaving the nest the young should be fully feathered but the beak will be still black or dark horn-colored.

When the young leave the nest they will continue to beg for food from other avian inhabitants as well as their own hard-working parents; sometimes the whole bird population of a mixed aviary will help feed the young Zebra Finches. Within 5 weeks the young are usually independent, and have learned their way to the food supply! Their beaks will have turned red by now and in a further 6 weeks they will be capable of breeding.

The conscientious breeder, however, would not allow such young birds to breed. It would only lead to unpleasantries in the form of weekly offspring or infertile eggs. It is best to wait until birds are 9 to 12 months old before breeding is allowed.

The Breeder's Role

The breeder who uses nest boxes can inspect the nests at regular intervals. However, it is wise not to disturb the nest too often until the birds are completely accustomed to the breeder. A good pair of Zebra Finches should have few problems and, in most cases will succeed in hatching and rearing a strong, healthy brood.

One method of keeping an eye on things is to operate your "breeding calendar" or record book properly. About three days after nest construction is finished, shine a flashlight in the nest or feel gently in the nest with a finger, to see if eggs are present, in which case you make a note of the date. Fourteen days later young should have hatched and closer inspection will be necessary. The time scale is usually precise but sometimes it can take a day or so longer, so do not be in too much of a hurry to discard eggs. Anyway, infertile eggs, or those in which the embryo has died, are usually removed by the parent birds.

Any eggs that fall from the nest can be recovered and returned to the nest as long as the shell is still intact. Eggs falling out repeatedly should however be discarded as they are almost bound to fail.

Make a note of the day the youngsters hatch as you will have to leg band (ring) them when they are 8 days old. After banding you will know that the young will leave the nest about 15 days later. By following these procedures you can thus keep an eye on what is happening with a minimum of nest inspections and ensure that the birds are disturbed as little as possible.

BREEDING RULES TO REMEMBER

- Zebra Finches and other Australian grass finches must be at least 9–10 months old before they are allowed to breed.

- Zebra Finches and other Australian grass finches can be used for breeding for 4–5, and sometimes up to 7 years.

- The minimum temperature during breeding must be 68°F (20°C); this temperature is also the minimum outside the breeding season!

- Be content with two, or at the most, three broods per pair, per breeding season.

- Always provide a minimum of two identical nest boxes per pair and put these in different places and heights (never lower than 6 feet (2 meters) in an aviary), preferably in the roofed part of the aviary.

- Serious incubation of the eggs usually starts after the third egg is laid. The incubation time averages 14 days. Both sexes take turns on the nest. The young leave the nest after 21–22 days and are usually quite independent after another 2 weeks.

It is very important to see that your birds never run short of food and water at this time. The food should be as varied as possible. Bath water should also be available and this should be renewed daily. A few nest inspections are good, as this is one way the fancier can learn more about his birds' breeding behavior; one of the most interesting aspects of the hobby. In the first place, a nest inspection will enable the breeder to detect and remove infertile eggs.

Feeding the Youngsters

The feeding of the newly fledged young is an exquisite sight. The youngster can turn its head almost 120 degrees; it squats low and begs loudly for food while moving the body backwards and forwards. The parent sticks its beak in the open bill of the fledgling and pumps it full with food. The parents carefully see that each youngster gets its fair share.

The screeching, begging tones of the young are only heard during the breeding season when the young are being raised. As soon as the birds are independent, it will cease. The sound not only stimulates the feeding response of the parents but seems also to stimulate the sex drive of other pairs of Zebra Finches.

As soon as the young are no longer fed by the parents, they should be removed to separate accommodations otherwise they are likely to interfere with the smooth running of consecutive broods. Moreover, there is a chance that they themselves will start breeding too early. Cocks and hens should preferably be separated, and allowed to mature in large cages or aviaries.

At the end of the breeding season, the best birds are selected for breeding the following season and paired up. A few more good birds are also kept for emergency, in case a bird or two is lost during the winter, bearing in mind that hens are not quite so robust and hardy as cocks and so a larger number of spare hens should be kept. All surplus stock is sold or given away to eager homes. These "extra" birds are not necessarily of poor quality, but perhaps not quite up to the mark and may be sold to help recover some expenses.

Problems

Though Zebra Finches are pretty low maintenance when it comes to breeding, you need to be on the look-out for a couple of problems that can occur.

"Egg Sandwich"

Sometimes after laying a few eggs a hen will fail to incubate properly and the pair will start building another nest on top of the original ("egg sandwich"). In fact three and even four nests are occasionally built on top of each other. Such a situation can arise when the pair is not properly compatible. When a hen is separated from her original partner and introduced to a new cock she will accept him eventually, but it can be some time before everything runs smoothly. This can take even longer if the hen can still see or hear her former partner.

There are various ways of preventing the construction of these "high-rise" nests. Firstly, only use adult, mature birds that are in first class condition for breeding. The nest boxes should not be too deep because the birds will often continue to build until the nest is level with the entrance. The third method is to remove all surplus nest material from the cage or aviary, as soon as the first clutch of eggs has been laid. The best way, of course, is to offer nesting facilities so the birds are forced to build a natural nest as they would in the wild.

Premature Fledging

The youngsters will fledge more readily in warm weather than in cold weather, however they cannot fly well enough to return to the nest and are likely to spend the night on the floor of the cage; if the weather should change they will end up shivering, will probably get chilled and most likely die. Such birds are best returned to the nest by the breeder the moment they are spotted. Premature fledging can often be prevented by using a well ventilated nest.

With colony breeding it can happen that a large number of young can fledge together. They will congregate together on the aviary floor and every time an adult Zebra Finch approaches it will be ambushed by a mob of screaming, begging chicks and will no longer be able to recognize its own offspring.

By limiting the numbers of breeding pairs per aviary such a situation can be minimized. Three or four pairs is best.

Fun
with Your
Zebra Finch

You'll enjoy your Zebra Finches for the cheerful bundles of energy they are; in fact, probably you'll find yourself enjoying them so much you'll want to increase your involvement with these birds. Many people find it is a small step from being a Zebra Finch owner to being a Zebra Finch enthusiast! There are  many projects you can undertake with your Zebra Finch. What is provided here is just a small overview, so if you decide you do want to expand your bird-related activities, follow up with some of the books listed in chapter 11.

Home, Sweet Home

A large cage is a fine way to keep a pair of Zebra Finches, but suppose you decide you want to breed your birds or want to keep more than one pair. Then you should consider providing more elaborate housing. A bird room and an aviary both have the advantages of providing more freedom and a more natural environment for your birds. Consider planning and building yourself or adapting a room in your home.

Consider building a bird room for your Zebra Finches with access to an outdoor aviary.

A BIRD ROOM

A very convenient size for a bird room would be about $12 \times 9 \times 6$ feet. This would be simple to keep warm and would hold a reasonable number of indoor shelters with access to outdoor flights.

Light and Heat

The average mean body temperature of most birds is around 10 degrees F higher than that of humans and we must try and find some means of providing something close to the type of climate they would experience in their natural habitat. Of course, if we want to spend a lot of money we can keep our birds in a heated, thermostatically controlled bird room. As most of us cannot afford such luxuries there is another cheaper way. The sun is free, and if we can use it in a special way this is ideal. Any bird room should preferably be built with the front or most open area facing to the south (in the northern hemisphere; of course the opposite would apply in the southern hemisphere). This orientation is to ensure that the room is heated by the sun's rays for the longest possible period each day. The sun will be enjoyed by the birds, and it is quite remarkable how even the weak winter sun can make a difference to the temperature of a correctly oriented room. Once your bird room is an effective sun catcher you will still need some means of retaining the heat. This is done with insulation. You can insulate the walls and ceiling and even the floor with similar materials to those used in your own home. Double glazed windows and tightly fitting doors will also be an asset.

*Nesting baskets
in the bird room
or aviary should
be filled to the
entrance with
nesting material.*

In spite of our preoccupation with maintaining warmth in the winter, we must not forget that adequate ventilation is also very important. High temperatures, unfortunately, tend to turn air stale much faster than cold air. Of course, air circulation in the summer needs to be more frequent than in the winter, but we must have a means of controlling ventilation throughout the year. One good method is to have regulated ventilation grills near the floor in each of the four walls and a rain-proof exhaust grill in the roof. The grill facing the pre-vailing wind should be closed to avoid drafts, and, when the wind changes, you just open or close what-ever grills are necessary. On cold or very windy days the grills can be partially to almost completely closed depending on the required temperature. It is advisable to use vermin proof grills or to cover them with fine wire mesh.

If you want to keep your birds in good condition and healthy throughout the winter, it will be necessary to provide a proper balance between heating and ventilation. Do not overheat in the winter as this may bring the birds into breeding condition too early. The best way is to try and maintain the inside temperature around 65 to 82 degrees F (18 to 28 degrees C), and allow access to an open flight cage so that the birds can decide for themselves where they want to be at any particular time. The higher inside temperature will soon attract the birds inside if it gets too cold outside!

Be sure to put screens on all the windows, so you can open them safely to let in fresh air and direct sunlight. This is of prime importance for your feathered friends. Paint the walls with washable paint in natural, quiet colors, like light green, light gray, pale blue and such.

These tiny Zebra Finches are the rewards of careful breeding.

Plants

Decorate the corners with live plants in pots and barrels, and install fabricated perches there, too. This way you preserve maximum flight space. You can consider planting elder, willow, roses, all types of philodendron, reeds, bamboo, privet or dwarf conifers. You will have to count on some damage inflicted by the birds, so you'll have to replace the plants now and then. You will need to spray the plants regularly with a mister. I consider a bird room complete only if proper attention has been given to plants. If you have a dense collection of plants, you have a good chance that many types of birds, even Zebra Finches, will build a nest there in the

open (a so-called free nest), which is highly interesting
in itself.

IDEAL ACCOMMODATIONS

An ideal situation is to have a bird room on the ground
floor with an outdoor aviary attached. On pleasant,
sunny, windless days, you can open the entrance to the
aviary, and the birds can enjoy fresh air and direct sunlight to their heart's content. Ultraviolet rays on the
feathers are beneficial, and birds that have been kept
indoors for a long winter improve visibly when they can
come back out into the open air and enjoy a daily s
un bath. The outdoor aviary should have plenty of
plantings, also, so birds can hide in the greens if they
need to.

Bird Shows

Another way to get more involved with your finch is to
enter bird shows. Before you can show your finch, however, you'll need to get a good idea about what's
involved in showing.

*Showing your
Zebra Finch can
be an exciting
and rewarding
hobby.*

To start, join a bird club and talk to other members
about showing you the ropes. You'll not only need
to learn about what goes on at these shows, you'll
need to learn what makes a winning bird. When you
attend shows, talk to the exhibitors about their birds,

Enjoying Your
Zebra Finch

especially those with winning entries. Learn what makes these birds stand out, and start to develop your own idea of winning quality.

The next step is to acquire your own show bird. Talk to owners of winning birds and ask if they have show birds for sale. Talk to breeders in your club and get recommendations for other breeders if they can't offer you the kind of bird you want.

At a bird show, the entries are displayed side by side in their cages, and the judges approach each cage checking for things like color, overall physical appearance and specific features considered important to the Zebra Finch. Because your bird will be displayed in its cage, presenting an attractive showcage is second in importance only to displaying a beautiful bird. First, make sure your show cage is clean. Not only will an unclean cage distract judges from your bird, it also reflects poorly on your talents as a birdkeeper. The cage should be painted a solid, bright color. A busy backdrop will interfere with the judge's ability to see your bird and evaluate it properly, and will not show off your bird to a great advantage. On the other hand, the striking colors of the Zebra Finch show up beautifully against a bright blue or green background.

SPRUCING UP YOUR BIRD ROOM

While a bird room would be nice with only basic perches and food and water vessels, take advantage of the extra space to create a complete environment for your finches. Place potted plants along the walls and in the corners. Good plants to keep in your bird room include roses, philodendron, dwarf evergreens, grass, bamboo and reeds. Painting the room a light color will make it seem sunnier. Place perches in the corners to allow for maximum flight room. Make sure the plants you include aren't poisonous and the other accessories are safe, but other than that, let your imagination be your guide!

Once you have promising show birds, you'll need to prepare them, and yourself, for the show season. Get your bird used to its exhibition cage and make it comfortable with different people approaching the cage by holding mock shows in your living room. Have different friends come up to the cage and look closely at the bird. In time, your bird will become used to this and will remain calm when it is approached by a stranger.

Next, consult with members of your club and check in publications like *Birdtalk* for listings of shows in your area. Call or write to the person listed to obtain a show catalogue and then go through it meticulously. Make a note of the check-in time and fees, as well as other important information like what category you will enter and who will be judging your category.

Make sure you treat the judges and other entries with due respect and pay close attention throughout the proceedings. There's a lot you can learn!

chapter 9

Other
Compatible
Finches

Diamond Firetailed and
Parson's finches

Of the nineteen known Australian grass finches, the following species are well-established in aviculture. They all are excellent partners for the Zebra Finch.

Spice Finch (*Lonchura punctulata*)

Length: 4 inches (10 centimeters)

This bird is practically always available. It is modest in its demands and is suitable for garden and large indoor aviaries. In the winter it must be housed indoors in a frost-free area, but this doesn't imply that this species cannot tolerate temperate zones. Experience has shown that, if the birds are given an outside aviary, with a sturdily build night enclosure (containing felt-lined nest boxes, which also serve as sleeping places), they can spend the winter outdoors. A pair builds a rather large, round nest in a thick bush. The bird comes in various subspecies and is found in India, Sri Lanka, southeastern Asia, south China, Taiwan and Hainan, through Greater and Lesser Sundas (except Borneo) to Sulawesi (formerly Celebes) and the Philippines; introduced into Australia in 1942.

Spice Finch.

Pictorella Finch (*Lonchura pectorallis*)

Length: 5 inches (12 centimeters)

Pictorella Finch.

This bird is rather rare in aviculture. The species is very friendly towards its keeper as well as towards other small birds. The mating dances of the male are performed on the ground; he dances around his future bride while bobbing his head and sometimes touching the hen's bill or picking in the sand. The wings are carried low and the tail goes from right to left. Newly

113

imported birds must be acclimatized with care at a temperature of about 77 degrees F (25 degrees C). Birds born in captivity are hardy but must be placed indoors when the temperature drops below 65 degrees F (18 C). The species is found in northwestern Australia and Northern Territory; in grassland and savannas, usually in extremely dry country. The nest in the wild is built low between grass clumps.

Chestnut-breasted Finch (*Lonchura castaneothorax*)

Length: 4 inches (10 centimeters)

Chestnut-breasted Finch.

This species is rarely available in the trade, although various European aviculturists are occasionally breeding this amicable bird in well planted (reeds!), large, outdoor aviaries with a variety of nesting boxes. Before the breeding starts, the male dances in front of his mate, drawing himself up to his full height, while hopping up and down on his branch or perch. This species is excellent for the beginner, but it must be said that they practically never breed. They are pleasant, tolerant birds that never get into arguments and bear up quite well in most circumstances. They also need fresh bath water daily, like Zebras, and nail care, like all the other Lonchura-species. The species comes from tropical north and east Australia, along the coast (near Sydney) in two subspecies; also in Papua New Guinea and Vulcan Island; introduced into New Caledonia,

Society Islands and Tahiti. Their habitat is grassland, cane fields, reed beds and along the coastal districts of northern Australia, where they live in sometimes large flocks. They often destroy whole cereal crops.

Star Finch (*Bathilda* [Neochmia] *ruficauda*)

Length: 4 inches (10 centimeters)

A pair of Star Finches.

This species is quite popular. The female is not easy to distinguish from the male, but with experience, sexing can be done quickly because the red on the throat of the female is less intense. Star Finches are easy to breed, provided they are kept in a well-planted, quiet aviary. For planting, select tall grass, reeds, ivy and dense bushes. The birds are exceptionally friendly to fellow inhabitants. In roomy outside aviaries, they usually will build a free nest in a little bush. Don't disturb them there, as they are quite sensitive. During fall and winter Star Finches must be housed indoors at room temperature.

Gouldian Finches (*Chloebia gouldiae*)

Length: 5 inches (12 centimeters)

In addition to the red-headed form, there is a black-headed form (most common in the wild) and a yellow-headed form (quite rare). This bird is the keystone of every serious collection. A single pair can be brought to breeding in a roomy cage, but they prefer garden or (especially) indoor aviaries. Gouldian Finches are pleasant toward other birds, and there is no reason not to house them with other Australian finches. The first molt occurs at 8 to 10 weeks; at 5 months, the young show adult colors.

Gouldian Finch.

Painted Fire-tailed Finch (*Emblema picta*)

Length: 4 inches (10 centimeters)

*Painted
Fire-tailed Finch.*

This is an extremely attractive bird, very suited to an aviary. It gets along well with other birds, including those of its own kind, and seldom fights. The aviary should be well planted, a requirement of all Australian grass finches. There should be open sandy spots as well. The birds tend to sleep on the ground or in low-hanging nest boxes. The birds build nests in the plantings or in nest boxes, like canary nest boxes, provided they are placed low to the ground. It tends to use rough nesting materials such as leaves, rough dry grass and bark, which are made into the foundation. The walls of the nest are made of small twigs, grass, leaf veins and the like. For padding on the inside, it uses all types of small, soft feathers. Nest building can take all of 2 weeks. The birds are found in the midwest and northwest of Australia, the Northern Territory, central Australia, the northern part of South Australia and the northwestern parts of Queensland.

Black-throated Finch (*Poephila cincta*)

Length: 4 inches (10 centimeters)

Black-throated Finch.

This is a sociable, but sometimes aggressive bird in captivity. A pair needs space; hence a large, well-planted aviary is necessary. Several pairs together (at least three pairs, never only two) stimulate social behavior and nest building. They build a bottle-like nest of grass, feathers and plant fibers, with an entrance tunnel, but prefer using a nest box or the old nests of other birds. The birds occur in Cape York to South Queensland and the New South Wales border, in three subspecies.

117

Long-tailed Finch (*Poephila acuticauda*)

Length: 7 inches (18 centimeters), including the tail

Long-tailed Finch.

Extremely sociable bird in the wild, but sometimes troublesome in an aviary. Can best be kept with larger birds in a well-planted aviary. They must be housed indoors during fall and winter. The female lays five to six eggs; the sexes alternate the incubating for 13 days. Give the birds as many different nest boxes as possible; they must be positioned high behind natural cover and far apart. They will construct roosting nests as well, so be sure to provide enough building materials. Sometimes different pairs will sleep together in those nests. The species lives in northern and northwestern Australia.

Masked Finch (*Poephila personata*)

Length: 5 inches, 12 centimeters)

This is an excellent sociable but noisy bird that needs a large, well-planted aviary. They live mainly on the ground in search for food, but spend their mating season high between the branches of dead scrub and trees. Their nest is bulky, close to the ground, and constructed from grass, small feathers, plant fibers and wool. In the nest-sites pieces of charcoal are incorporated (for hygroscopic reasons). This species lives in northern Australia. The subspecies P. p. leucotis or White-eared Grass Finch, with some white under the eye, is confined to the east coast of the Gulf on Cape York.

Masked Finch.

Bicheno's Finch (*Stizoptera* [Poephila] *bichenovii*)

Length: 3 to 4 inches (8 to 10 centimeters)

Bicheno's Finch.

This bird is also known as the Owl Finch. This is an extremely friendly and peaceful bird that must be housed indoors during fall and winter. They are often found on the ground, and it is advisable to have a leaf-mold compost heap in one of the corners. This heap should give the birds the opportunity to look for insects and satisfy their urge for scratching. This species builds its own little nests from grass and feathers in thick shrubbery, or uses a nesting box. In addition to insects, standard seed mixtures are needed. The subspecies with the black rump is scientifically named S. b. annulosa and lives in the Northern Territory and the northwestern parts of Australia. The Bicheno's Finch lives in eastern New South Wales, Queensland (except the southwestern parts), northern areas of Northern Territory and northwestern Western Australia. In the wild both subspecies cross-breed.

Owl Finches.

Diamond Finch (*Zonaeginthus* [Emblema] *guttata*)

Length 5 inches (12 centimeters)

This species is not always very active in small cages and aviaries, where they usually become fat and pugnacious. They are therefore only suitable for large, well-planted facilities, together with other large finches. They are somewhat aggressive, especially during the breeding season. Never house two pairs in the same cage or aviary. Temperatures below 60 degrees F (15 degrees C) are not well taken; birds housed in outdoor quarters must be put inside as soon as temperatures start to drop in early fall. Pairs need a good selection of nesting materials: coconut fibers, leaf veins, wool, moss, and soft dry grass (up to 20 inches [50 centimeters] long!), but watch out for long pieces of thread and string, since the parents and young can get tangled in it. A free-standing bullet-shaped nest is usually constructed in a thick bush; the nest often has a long entrance tunnel. The birds also use various nest boxes. While one of the birds sets on the eggs or is

Diamond Finch.

feeding the youngsters, the other partner often makes nest repairs. The hen lays five to six eggs which are incubated by both parents for 12 to 14 days. The young leave the nest after approximately 30 days; about 2 weeks later they are already independent and must then be housed in a separate flight, as the male parent often aggressively chases them around. On the other hand, Diamond Finches are rather sensitive birds, so they won't always accept their partner. It is therefore advisable to let the birds do the choosing. In the wild they can be found in southern central Queensland, eastern New South Wales to Victoria and South Australia, and Kangaroo Island.

part four

Beyond
the
Basics

chapter 10

Resources

Magazines

A.F.A. Watchbird
3118 W. Thomas Road, #713
Phoenix, AZ 85017
(602)484-0931

Bird Breeder Magazine
P.O. Box 420235
Palm Coast, FL 32142-0235

Bird Talk
P.O. Box 57347
Boulder, CO 80323-7347

Caged Bird Hobbyist
7L. Dundas Circle
Greensboro, NC 27499-0765

Finch & Canary World
850 Park Avenue
Monterey, CA 93940
(800) 864-2500

Societies

American Federation of Aviculture
3118 W. Thomas Road, #713
Phoenix, AZ 85017
(602) 484-0931

Association of Avian Vetetrinarians
5770 Lake Worth Road
Lake Worth, FL 33463-3299

Avicultural Society of America, Inc.,
P.O. Box 2196
Redondo Beach, CA 90218

National Finch and Softbilled Society (NFSS)
c/o Ms. Lynda Bakula
P.O. Box 3232
Ballwin, MO 63022
(314) 394-3530

Recommended Reading

Bates, Henry and Busenbark, Robert. *Finches and Soft-billed Birds.* Neptune City: T.F.H. Publications, Inc.

Burgmann, Petra, D.V.M. *Feeding Your Pet Birds.* Hauppauge: Barron's Educational Series, Inc., 1993.

Gallerstein, G., D.V.M. *The Complete Bird Owner's Handbook.* New York: Howell Book House, 2nd Edition, 1994.

Kelsey-Wood, Dennis. *Finches as a Hobby.* Neptune City: T.F.H. Publications, Inc. 1995.

Koepff, Christa. *The New Finch Handbook.* Hauppauge: Barron's Educational Series, Inc., 1984.

Martin, Hans. *Zebra Finches.* Hauppauge: Barron's Educational Series, Inc., 1985.

Mobbs, A. J. *Complete Book of Australian Finches.* Neptune City: T.F.H. Publications, Inc.

Vriends, Matthew M., Ph.D. *Gouldian Finches.* Hauppauge: Barron's Educational Series, Inc., 1995.

Vriends, Matthew M., Ph.D. *Hand-feeding and Raising Baby Birds.* Hauppauge: Barron's Educational Series, Inc., 1996.